Vernacular Architecture of the Lake Counties

Vernacular
Architecture
of the

Lake
Counties

A field handbook by **R. W. Brunskill**

Faber and Faber
3 Queen Square
London

First published in 1974
by Faber and Faber Limited, 3 Queen Square, London WC1
Printed in Great Britain
by Alden and Mowbray Limited, Osney Mead, Oxford
All rights reserved

ISBN 0 571 09460 0

---

1. (*frontispiece*)
The Troutbeck Valley,
Westmorland

By the same author:
Illustrated Handbook of Vernacular Architecture

Preface and Acknowledgments

I first became aware of the qualities of vernacular architecture when, as a boy, I spent summers on the farm occupied by my grandparents which I now know to have one of the earliest dated examples of a bank barn, and which I recognised, even then, to be located in a district where there was a variety of building materials in use in rather precisely described localities, in the Eden Valley. I visited the farms of other relations in the same district and became dimly aware of further differences in planning and construction of farmhouses and layout and distribution of farm buildings. Days spent wandering on the fells led to the discovery of lime kilns, examples of industrial vernacular architecture, in the most unlikely places. All this I now know to have been part of the study of vernacular architecture; at that time it seemed part of a changeless rhythm of rural life.

My own interest in vernacular architecture has developed and my involvement in its study has deepened as time and circumstances have permitted. Within the School of Architecture of Manchester University I have been able to continue the work begun by Professor R. A. Cordingley and expanded by several of his colleagues. As a member of the Vernacular Architecture Group I have had my own knowledge of the subject and the techniques of its study sharpened through exposure in agreement and controversy to the keen minds of scholars too numerous to mention. As a lecturer I have been able through summer schools and extra-mural classes to pass on some of my own accumulated knowledge to others who were keen to develop interests often roused in much the same way as my own.

One result of the developing study was the publication of my *Illustrated Handbook of Vernacular Architecture*. This was intended to help the 'enthusiastic amateur' both to embark on systematic recording of examples in the field and to begin his understanding of the meaning of the records – extensive, intensive, and documentary – which he had collected. The *Illustrated Handbook* has been well received and appears to be reasonably successful in meeting its limited objectives. It was, however, obvious from the start that a single small handbook

Preface and Acknowledgments

intended for national use could give very limited help in elucidating the mysteries of the variety of vernacular architecture region by region, let alone those of the intricate variety district by district, almost parish by parish, which is one of the glories of this country. It was agreed, therefore that a series of regional handbooks should be prepared, and that they should concentrate on those regions, usually based on national parks where field studies generally are developing so rapidly and are proving so rewarding. The Lake Counties was the obvious region for the first handbook in the series.

Although I have taken most of the photographs and prepared all the diagrams specifically for this book, its preparation would have been quite impossible without the published work of which the principal items are noted in the list of references and recommendations for further reading. Its preparation would have been more difficult had I not had access to the unpublished work of the late Dr. J. E. Partington, of D. R. Moorhouse, of T. K. J. Eland, and of other former students of the University of Manchester School of Architecture, and to the unpublished thesis of Neil Birdsall, formerly of the Leeds School of Architecture. I am very grateful for the opportunity of having access to that material. I am also grateful to Dr. J. D. Marshall and M. Davies-Shiel for their help and interest particularly in the study of industrial buildings in the Lake Counties and for allowing me to make use of their researches. Some of the material was collected with the aid of the Neale Bursary and a Research Grant of the Royal Institute of British Architects. I would also like to acknowledge the help gained in discussions over many years from friends and colleagues, especially Dr. E. A. Gee, Sir Robert Hall, E. A. Mercer, Dr. T. L. Marsden, R. W. McDowall, T. M. Owen, J. T. Smith, P. Smith, and Dr. R. B. Wood-Jones; and also members of the Cumberland and Westmorland Antiquarian and Archaeological Society, especially the late C. M. L. Bouch, C. R. Hudleston, J. Hughes, and Professor G. P. Jones. I am very grateful to Alec Clifton-Taylor for reading the manuscript and making many helpful suggestions.

Finally I must thank my wife for her help in draft typing and her general forbearance during field work and writing, many relations and friends for hospitality, Mrs. M. Woodcock and Mrs. C. Blake for their expert typing, and, once again, Peter Crawley and his colleagues.

Wilmslow, Cheshire,
November 1972

Contents

List of illustrations

8

Introduction

This book is intended for use in the field by all those who wish to increase their understanding and appreciation of the ordinary buildings which are so important in the scenery of the Lake Counties.

In the field it is hoped that it will prove useful to both residents and visitors: to residents by helping them to understand the history and traditions of the district in which many of them have chosen to settle, demonstrating the range of uniformity and variety to be found in a compact apparently homogeneous region; to visitors whether teachers, students, or simply tourists, by helping them to understand one element in the total environment and cultural situation which has encouraged their journey, and by providing a basis of comparison with the buildings of their own locality. The handbook should be especially useful to those who wish to make a systematic study of some part of the region, for, in the study of vernacular architecture one may see the interplay of topographical, geological, climatic, historical and economic factors in developments which are still proceeding – as witness the conversion of barns originally intended for the hand flail threshing of a yeoman's corn and adapted to accommodate the hay of a stock-rearing tenant farmer into the weekend and retirement houses of families whose own ancestors may have left the same district as part of the flight from the land a century ago! It is hoped that the observations of the resident or visitor and the field studies of the student will be all the more rewarding if based on a suggested framework of observation.

As this is a field handbook the illustrations form a substantial part of the contents. The drawings illustrating each plan-type or constructional detail are based on actual examples though not usually on a single identifiable building. The photographs include buildings now demolished as well as those still in private occupation; as the houses of working farmers they are not normally open to the public, though they are usually visible from the public roads and paths. Actual examples may be checked against the types illustrated and their characteristics compared, plans, materials, construction and details being related to the typical examples, their periods of use, and the districts in which they are usually found.

This handbook has been designed for use in conjunction with the *Illustrated Handbook of Vernacular Architecture* which has already been published and the other regional handbooks which are in preparation. The *Illustrated Handbook* suggested a sequence of observation of vernacular buildings in England and Wales and illustrated the main building materials, methods of construction, plan types, architectural details, etc., likely to be met, and included notes on how extensive surveys, intensive investigation by measured drawing and further enquiry into documentary sources could be made. This field handbook takes observation and study a stage further; it allows that after some preliminary investigation into the vernacular buildings of some part of the region a more detailed comparison of characteristics and deeper enquiry can be made into plan types, details of construction, and the use of architectural decoration on doors and windows and within the buildings. Field handbooks for other regions, being organised on similar lines, will help comparison between regions, assessing the wide variety of characteristics to be observed in a country as complex in its geography and history as Britain without neglecting the surprising degree of uniformity to be detected, different regions giving evidence of common trends.

Much of the information included in this book is condensed from the more detailed studies I have made in the Eden Valley and the Solway Plain. Many districts remain to be studied and all those which have once been covered in detail deserve further attention as more hidden items are revealed and as the developing study of vernacular architecture shows us all how much there is still to discover. The two 'vernacular trails', for the contrasting villages of Troutbeck and Milburn suggest what can be seen simply by walking through a community. The suggestions for further work at the end of the book indicate possible lines of systematic study which, if properly conducted and published, would justify the definitive study of vernacular architecture which the Lake Counties deserve.

References are to the present counties of Cumberland (C), Westmorland (W) and Lancashire (L) which will form the new county of Cumbria.

2. Sketch map of the Lake Counties showing land over 1000 ft.

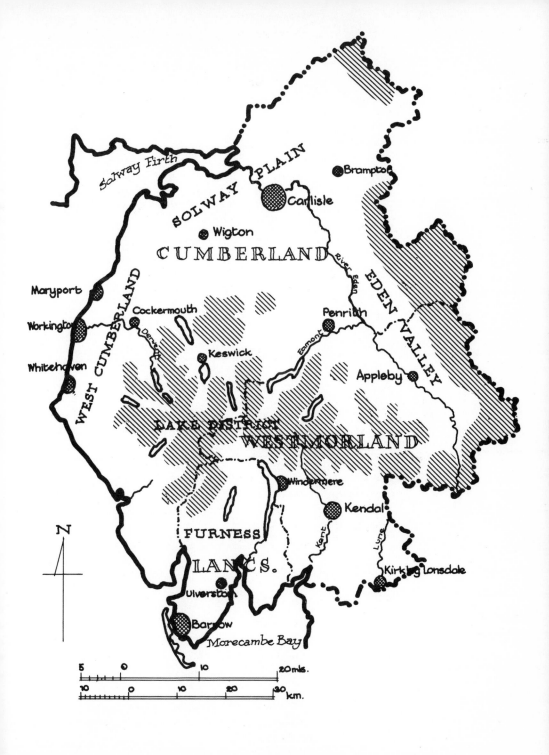

Solway Firth

SOLWAY PLAIN

● Brampton

● Carlisle

● Wigton

CUMBERLAND

EDEN VALLEY

River Eden

Maryport ●

WEST CUMBERLAND

Cockermouth ●

Penrith ●

Workington ●

Derwent

Keswick ●

Eamont

Whitehaven ●

Appleby ●

LAKE DISTRICT

WESTMORLAND

● Windermere

Kent

● Kendal

N

FURNESS

Lune

LANCS.

Kirkby Lonsdale ●

Ulverston ●

● Barrow

Morecambe Bay

5   0   10   20 mls.

10   0   10   20   30 km.

The Region and its Study

The region covered – the Lake Counties – comprises Cumberland, Westmorland and Lancashire-north-of-the-Sands. It includes the Lake District as generally understood and as defined by the boundary of the Lake District National Park, but it also includes a broad peripheral band: the narrow south-facing valleys of the Lune, Kent, Keer, etc., the early-industrialised valleys of Furness, the broad but blighted coastal strip of West Cumberland, and the rich sheltered Eden Valley, protected by the Lake District, precisely defined by the Pennines and at one time containing a major part of the population and its architectural effort in the region.

The building types included are, of course, vernacular rather than polite in quality, and predominantly domestic and rural. They are 'vernacular' – the products of local craftsmen meeting simple functional requirements according to traditional plans and procedures and with the aid of local building material and constructional methods, rather than 'polite' – the efforts of professional designers, meeting the more elaborate needs of a formal way of life with the aid of internationally accepted rules and procedures, advanced constructional techniques, and materials chosen for aesthetic effect rather than local availability. The domestic buildings exclude the Great Houses (never very numerous) of the nobility, great landowners, and other men of provincial or national importance, but include the Large Houses of the local gentry, squirearchy, or the most important of the tenant farmers, the Small Houses of the great bulk of farmers (customary tenants, 'statesmen', yeomen, or leaseholders) and the Cottages of the poor, the landless labourers, artisans, widows, etc. With the domestic buildings are included some farm buildings – barns, cow-houses, stables, granaries, etc., and some early industrial buildings such as mills, furnaces, kilns and factories. Examples are predominantly rural, reflecting the former distribution of population and enterprise, and the present-day survival of recognisable examples, but with attention drawn to the rather different character shown in urban vernacular even in the Lake Counties.

The period covered ranges from about 1350 to about 1850. Before the middle of the 14C the few buildings erected of materials permanent enough to survive were churches, castles, or the fortified houses of men powerful in Church or State, and so of little vernacular content; after about 1850, even the humblest houses were beginning so to conform to national standards of planning, construction, and taste, that their vernacular interest is much reduced. In agricultural and industrial buildings the period covered is rather different; virtually no examples survive earlier than the late 17C and traditional designs continued in use almost to the end of the 19C.

Within the three broad categories of domestic vernacular buildings: Large Houses, Small Houses, and Cottages, examples have been illustrated from different parts of a Vernacular Zone lying between Vernacular and Polite Thresholds. In a graph of status and time the Polite Threshold separates buildings high in vernacular content from those classified as 'polite' in architecture; thus in the late 14C such few Great Houses as existed were designed with national rather than local precedent in mind, in the late 16C the same comment could be applied to many Large Houses, in the late 18C practically all Large Houses were polite rather than vernacular in quality, while a hundred years later many farmhouses and even some cottages had lost all trace of vernacular characteristics. The Vernacular Threshold indicates that there is a period from which many examples survive for investigation, and an earlier 'Dark Age' whose vernacular buildings can only be studied through documents or by excavation. This period varies with social status and in the Lake Counties the Large Houses of the 14C and 15C, the Small Houses of the 17C and the Cottages of the 18C and 19C may be placed on the vernacular threshold. They materialised as fully developed designs; whole villages are full of houses of the 17th, 18th and 19th centuries with no trace of their predecessors. Between the two thresholds the Vernacular Zone offers profitable study of Large Houses from mid 14C to mid

3. Diagram showing the Vernacular Zone for domestic architecture in the Lake Counties based on approximately 200 dated examples from all parts of the region. Below the Vernacular Threshold no examples survive, above the Polite Threshold examples lack significant vernacular qualities. The dates are those which appear on the buildings, the position on the scale of size-types is based on my own assessment

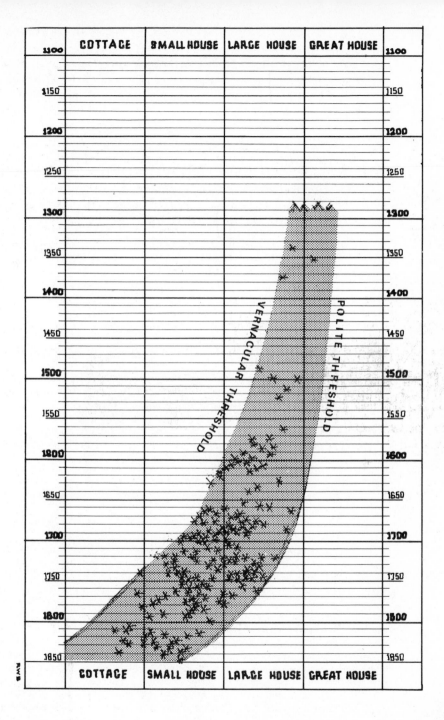

18C; Small Houses from mid 17C to mid 19C and Cottages from mid 18C to mid 19C or a little later.

While the *Illustrated Handbook of Vernacular Architecture* stressed building materials and methods of construction, this, and other Regional Handbooks, will instead stress the plan types which have been distinguished through study of domestic and other buildings. However, the characteristics of various walling materials used, such as sandstone or clay, and roofing materials such as stone flags or slate, together with cruck construction and the derived types of roof truss, will be described. Architectural details such as the shape and decoration of doors and windows will be described and illustrated; they are very

4. Example analysed
This is a brief analysis of the characteristics which may be observed from the outside of a small house such as this one at Gt. Orton, Cumberland (demolished in 1961).
a. walls of clay, rendered and whitewashed; walls of lower end red sandstone rubble, not coursed
b. gabled roof
c. verge is masked by corrugated roof covering
d. eaves also masked
e. present corrugated roof covering, though its pitch and eaves and verge details almost certainly conceals earlier thatch
f. ridge masked by later covering
g. chimneys at each gable, modern brick, forward of ridge
h. some indication of corbelled brick water tabling
i. no dormer windows
j. relative positions of main door, 'fire window', chimney stack, and other windows suggest a two-unit and cross-passage plan. As the lower end has been rebuilt it is difficult to decide whether it was downhouse or farm buildings. A room of clay and thatch at the upper end may have been used for domestic industry
k. two-storey section, though with upper floor rooms partly in roof space
l. not visible externally, but staircase rises from within the parlour
m. window shape square generally though with one narrow fire window and another narrow balancing window, at least one later window upstairs; all original windows have chamfered stone dressings and may have had square cut mullions
n. window frames generally wood fixed casement with individual opening lights
o. door has sandstone dressings and chamfered jambs, rings presumably for tethering horses
p. the original door has been replaced
q. buildings at lower end rebuilt, served as scullery but blocked doorway from cross-passage suggest possible earlier use as cow-house
Plan: 1. cross-passage, 2. living room, 3. parlour, 4. weaving room (?), 5. added lean-to scullery and 6 dairy, 7. staircase, 8. loft with two upper cruck trusses, 9. outhouses with blocked access from cross-passage

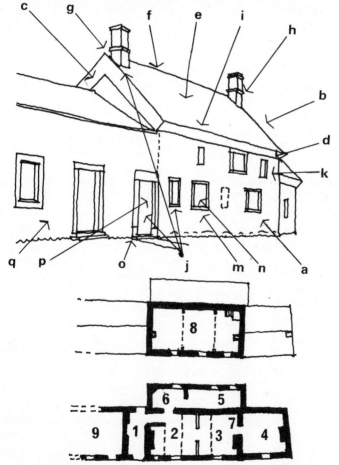

useful aids to dating both because nationally popular details were used, after an interval, in the Lake Counties and because there is an unusually high proportion of dated buildings, especially from the late 17C onwards. Actual buildings may be checked against time scales. As no single criterion is an accurate guide to a building's date these several characteristics will be briefly described and illustrated so that planning, construction and detailing of a building under study may all contribute information whereby its probable history can be established.

Within the compass of a field handbook only a limited amount can be added to what is gathered in the field by individual observers. Some aspects of vernacular architecture have already attracted attention and the notes list books and articles which will help the reader to extend his investigations. However, comparatively little with a direct bearing on the subject has been written and even less has been published. It is hoped that a real pioneering spirit, examining and recording buildings to extract information which if not gathered now may be lost for ever, adding to the common fund of knowledge by adding to the short list of publications, will increase the pleasure of visiting the Lake Counties.

Topography, climate, geology

Cumbria, the Lake Counties, consists of the ancient counties of Cumberland (about 1,500 sq. miles in area), and Westmorland (about 800 sq. miles) together with the detached portion of Lancashire north of Morecambe Bay and sometimes given the name Furness District from the name of one of its parts. The Lake Counties make a compact geographical entity, limited by the Scottish Border in the north-east, limited generally by the watershed of the Pennines in the east and south-east, and by the coast of the Irish Sea elsewhere, ranging from Morecambe Bay in the south to the Solway Firth in the north. Around the central dome of the Lake District there lie the broad funnel-shaped Eden Valley, widening out to the Solway Plain, the narrower valleys or dales which drain the main part of the mountainous hub, the dissected upland of Furness, and the rather narrow, isolated, coastal belt of West Cumberland.

The varied topography and consequent scenic attraction of the region is too well known to require much comment. The basic rock formations of the Lake District, laid bare by glaciation, give an Alpine grandeur out of all proportion to their small size. The steep-sided dales gouged out by glaciers provide text-book examples of hanging valleys, coombes, erratics, etc., with long narrow lakes and circular isolated tarns in the centre of the region and small steep-sided hillocks, the drumlins and eskers, scattering on the plain at the periphery. The rivers, fed by the melting snow of the Ice Ages and still sustained by locally high rainfall, have deposited silt to make deltas within the valleys such as that which splits Bassenthwaite from Derwentwater and along the coast where embankments and barrages have been used to reclaim this fertile land. The sea, advancing and receding through time, has worn away great cliffs as at St. Bees Head but has also retreated to leave terraces and ridges as along the coast between Maryport and Silloth. The Eden Valley is dominated by the steep cliff face of the Great Whin Cill, running along the Pennine slopes; as the valley narrows between Appleby and Brough the surrounding hills appear bleak and forbidding but in the opposite direction the widening vale appears gentler, more humane, though at times, as when the River Eden scores out its deep gorge at Wetheral towards Carlisle, hardly less dramatic. Man's effect on the scenery has been mixed. Drainage and reclamation have created green fields out of dank bogs and coastal marshes; hedges and walls, farm clusters and villages, have given scale to the hills; but slag heaps and worked-out iron mines, derelict machinery and sprawling industrial estates have scarred the West Coast.

The Lake Counties lie between latitudes 54° and 55° North (similar to the southern part of Labrador and almost the latitude of Moscow) but they show considerable climatic variation. The average annual rainfall ranges from less than 30 inches at the mouth of the River Eden to almost 180 inches at Styhead Tarn. The greater part of the Eden Valley and the Solway Plain has less than 35 inches a year but the Lake District has everywhere more than twice as much. In spite of the northern latitude, much of the region, especially the southern coastal valleys, is remarkably mild in winter and because of the latitude the long summer days can give creditable averages of sunshine. Little snow falls in the southern valleys but on the Lake District mountains it can lie for a month at a time and on the Pennines to the east for even longer. The former railway line across Stainmore was regularly blocked and the line to Alston was saved from closure for a long time lest the town be cut off during the winter. The climate is favourable to both cultivation and stock rearing in the Eden Valley and Solway Plain, rather less so but more favourable to fruit growing in Furness, quite inhospitable over all the Lake District even in the valley bottoms where cold frost-laden air collects, and bleak in the high Pennine fells and east Cumberland.

21

Geology and topography march closely together in the Lake Counties. The dome of the Lake District consists of old hard slates and granites. These are almost surrounded by a belt of carboniferous limestone reaching the sea in South Westmorland and Furness and embracing the Eden Valley to range along the length of the Pennines. The West Cumberland coast and the floor of the Eden Valley consists of sandstone, partly hard and pink but mainly the soft brown Permian and Triassic of Penrith and St. Bees. The Solway Plain has marl and lias deposits with alluvium from the rivers. In the Lake District the basic rocks are generally exposed or covered with a thin sprinkling of soil; on the perimeter they lie beneath the glacial drift of clay, sand, and morainic rubbish.

History

In the strictest sense, the surviving remnants of prehistoric structures are examples of vernacular building if not vernacular architecture and there is considerable evidence of early settlement in the Lake Counties, so much that the archaeologists sometimes find it difficult to distinguish between prehistoric huts, medieval houses and post-medieval shielings when arranging their excavations. But generally history, and certainly intensive historical research, begins with the arrival of the Romans. They occupied the region as a military zone for nearly four centuries, established forts, camps, signal stations, and civilian settlements, and left behind in Hadrian's Wall a permanent monument to their building skill, or at least one as permanent as the picks of nearby masons and the ploughs of generations of farmers would permit.

After the departure of the Romans near the end of the 4th century AD we assume that the native inhabitants and settled colonists maintained a semi-Roman civilization under their Arthurian heroes, but this was broken down first by Saxon pressure through Furness and South Westmorland, then by Danish expansion over Stainmore and along the river valleys, next by settlement of Norsemen moving during the 10th century from their bases in Ireland and the Isle of Man up the creeks and channels of the Solway Firth, Morecambe Bay, and the Cumberland Coast, and finally, though not until after 1092, by the spread of the Norman pattern of church and state organisation. Even then the Scottish Crown held Carlisle for thirty years during the middle of the 12C and was granted manors around Inglewood Forest in Cumberland for even longer. The last segment of frontier between the two nations was not established until the division of the Debateable Land in 1552.

The Domesday Survey included only those southern parts of the Lake Counties which were considered to be part of England. As the frontier was pushed north during the 12C and 13C the region was divided into baronies such as Liddell and Burgh, Appleby and Kendal, each one with its castle. Eventually the counties of Cumberland and Westmorland were established and divided into wards, though the distinction between the Appleby and Kendal baronies of Westmorland reflected a geographical difference which still affects county administration. The pattern of church organisation during the early medieval period included very large empty parishes with tiny parish churches as well as the smaller more conventional parishes of the less sparsely settled districts; they were divided between the diocese of Carlisle, set up in 1133, and the Archdeaconry of Richmond in the diocese of York, which encompassed the whole southern part of the region. There were fewer than a dozen monastic establishments, of which Holm Cultram, Shap, and Furness were of some small local account, but these few did provide a focus of culture and economic enterprise in a poor, lonely, and exposed part of the kingdom.

Throughout the 13C there was peace between England and Scotland and the border counties enjoyed some relative prosperity, but the opening of the 14C began a long unsettled period. The attempt made by Edward I at the conquest of Scotland crystallised a sense of patriotism in that country which was later to justify raids and invasion campaigns far into the Lake Counties. There were short periods of peace during which the local economy could recover but in the 15C the Wars of the Roses added internal strife to the local feuds and international campaigns.

Two centuries of confusion were terminated by strong Tudor government. A reconciliation of sorts was made with Scotland; the power of the Marcher Barons was reduced as the offices of Wardens of the Marches were strengthened, the opposing wardens being accountable to their respective monarchs. Raids continued but were limited in extent and subject to an agreed set of rules. Temporal order was marred by the spiritual disorder of the Reformation and the Lake Counties suffered from the unsuccessful conservative rebellions of 1536 and 1596. Whatever the national benefit of the Dissolution of the Monasteries might have been there is no doubt that its local economic and cultural results were tragic.

Economically, local peace was affected by national decline in the value of money. It has been estimated that the cost of living at the end of the 16th century was five times that at the beginning. Then as now, inflation inhibited the accumulation of wealth by landowners and benefited protected tenants. There was pressure by the landowning families to erode the traditional rights of the customary tenants; in so far as this pressure was successfully resisted there was an increase in the prosperity of the yeoman class. The opportunity to improve holdings by enclosure was not generally taken at this time either by hard-pressed landlords or prosperous tenants, and even after the Plagues of 1568 and 1569, the traditional agricultural methods were generally maintained.

The opening of the seventeenth century gives an opportunity to mention the system of farming. As might be expected from the history and position of the region, agriculture was related as much to the Scottish as English methods. On each manor there were open fields in which strips were held by the farmers, but these strips were not changed in rotation year by year, nor was there a rotation of field by field, one field lying fallow while others were cultivated. Instead the open field or 'townfield' represented the 'infield' of the Scottish system of cultivation. This field received all the manure and was cropped year after year. Other fields were permanent meadow, cropped for hay in June, left idle as the second crop of 'fog' grass grew, then used in pasture. The remaining land, and here the remainder was very extensive, was the 'outfield'. Occasionally parts of the outfield would be cultivated and a crop or two taken, but generally it was 'stinted', each farmer having the right to pasture a certain number of beasts throughout the year. On the eastern fellsides at least, some sort of transhumance was practised, flocks and herds being taken to the upper slopes and tended by the herdsmen who lived in temporary 'shielings' for this purpose. Even to the present day the un-enclosed fellsides are stinted with traditional allotments of pasture rights to each farm. As there was no rotation of holdings in the townfields, enclosure of a sort could and did take place from an early date; the 'rigg' or 'ridge' between the 'dales', 'furlongs', 'runs' or cultivated fields, being free from the plough, could carry a hedge or rough stone wall. Even now, the small narrow fields stretching out from the villages can be quite clearly distinguished. On these various fields oats were the principal crop and cows (nolt), sheep and small sturdy horses (nags) were pastured.

The Union of the Crowns in 1603 promised, and eventually secured, removal of the greatest cause of insecurity in the

region. The new extension of Scottish influence was held by
certain families on the Scottish side of the Border to give licence
for further raids on the English, but James I forcibly corrected
this illusion. The moss-troopers, Grahams, Armstrongs, Hether-
ingtons and the rest, offering no reliable allegiance to either
crown felt themselves unaffected by the political settlement, but
strong measures by the civil authorities on both sides of Liddel
Water, and especially by Lord William Howard of Naworth led
to summary justice for the elders of each clan and transportation
to Ireland at the expense of grateful landowners for the rest.

This slight but welcome reduction in the population was quite
counter to the trend in the 18th century and the early part of the
19th. It has been estimated that the population of Cumberland
doubled between 1688 and 1801 and increased by a third again
between 1801 and 1821, this increase occurring largely through
reduction of the mortality rate from disease, though partly
through some increase in birth rate. The improvement in hous-
ing conditions which will be observed during this span would
surely play a significant part in the improvement in health.

The increase in population was not uniform throughout the
county, the mining areas, industrial towns, and ports showing a
very high rate of increase, no doubt through migration from the
rural areas. The lower rate of increase outside the towns was
accompanied by changes in the methods of agriculture, increase
in the number and size of farms as a result of enclosures and
improved farming methods, and a more than proportionate
reduction in the number of yeomen, though 37% of farmers in
1829 were still recorded as of this class.

At the opening of the 18th century, the condition of agriculture in the region was considered to be backward in comparison
with the rest of the country. Traditional methods of cultivation
remained in use and centuries of inadequate rotation and
insufficient variety of crops together with unselective breeding
of animals, themselves of poor quality, contrasted with innova-
tions of the scientific farmers of the south and east of England.
During the century, however, the situation improved, largely
through the guidance of Dr. Graham of Netherby in methods of
drainage, manuring, and enclosure of land, and of J. C. Curwen
in the breeding of cattle and the variety of fodder.

In the region as elsewhere in the North the pace of the new
phase of enclosure was quickened through the division of open
land by agreement and by Act of Parliament. During this period
the tall drystone walls which march up the fells, dividing the
slopes into large square fields, were erected in a concentrated

endeavour which is still the wonder of visitors from the South.

By the turn of the century, observers praised the agricultural landscape of the Eden Valley and Solway Plain, contrasting the wide productive fields and industrious labourers with the stunted crops and slothful farmers of earlier generations. While this change contributed to the general good, it was not always so satisfactory for the individual family.

Generations of socialist historians have pointed out the disadvantages of family labour and domestic industry but the dialect verse of the Cumberland parishes contrasts the happy days of the village life and personal charity with the less understanding bureaucracy of the Union overseer. If the continued increase of population is a fair test of improvement, however, it must be admitted that the gain outweighed the loss.

The beginnings of industry noted in the 17th century flourished in the 18th though with a predominantly agricultural economy. The south-western part of the region shared in the development of coal mining as in West Cumberland and in iron working and smelting as in Furness, to become one of the wonders of the age. Aspatria, a village of about 300 people in 1801, had quadrupled in size 50 years later. The outcrops of coal on Tindale Fell and on Stainmore continued to be worked for local use; Britton reported the adoption of the latest form of mechanisation in 'a railed wagon-way which the Earl of Carlisle has lately made from his collieries at Tindale Fell'. Water power, and later steam, transformed the domestic textile industry of the districts round Carlisle and Kendal into a factory system, principally of cottons, and based on Wigton, Dalston, Brampton, etc., as well as the large towns. Dalston had four cotton mills, two corn mills, and a forge by 1829. The beginning of a tourist industry may be observed at Allonby, which in 1748 'had a considerable concourse for bathing by the sea'.

Improvements in agriculture and industry were accompanied by improvements in transport. Turnpike roads were established to give some sort of a road system suitable for vehicles and with Carlisle as its focus. A canal serving Kendal was opened in 1819 and another was cut in 1819–23 to join Carlisle with what was intended to be its new port just east of Bowness. But the venture was not a success; the sea channel shifted, ships increased in size, eight locks in eleven miles slowed down the boats, and within five years the newly invented steam railways began to supersede canals. It had been proposed that Carlisle and Newcastle should be joined by canal but instead a railway was authorised in 1828 and, unprecedented engineering obstacles having been overcome, the Pennines were conquered by steam five years later. In 1846 the railway line joining Carlisle and Maryport was opened. In the same year Carlisle was joined by rail to London. The long isolation of the Lake Counties was over.

Large Houses

Introduction

Large Houses, the dwellings of families of provincial or considerable local importance, began to appear, constructed in permanent materials, in the late 14C, survive in substantial numbers from the 16C and 17C, but pass over the polite threshold, out of the vernacular zone during the late 18C and early 19C. Early examples, especially those in the northern and eastern parts of the Lake Counties, include substantial provision for refuge or defence, but later examples, especially those built after the Union of the Crowns of England and Scotland, tend to follow the patterns set with increasing uniformity over the whole country. Little is known of the design and construction of Large Houses erected before the use of permanent materials or of the impermanent domestic buildings erected within defensive enclosures or alongside towers or other refuges, but presumably a timber version of the hall with single or double cross wings was used. Large Houses were also usually farmhouses; the dwelling was only one element of a complex of buildings of which early flimsy versions have disappeared but of which substantial remains survive from the late 16C and 17C onwards. By the standards of wealthier counties these Large Houses are far from large in size or expensive in appearance.

Tower houses

The tower house has attracted a good deal of romantic interest and a train of legend as well as some serious study. No example survives intact but discarding subsequent alterations or reconstructing from ruins it is clear that in its complete form a tower house consisted of several floors of domestic accommodation housed within walls of defensible thickness – four feet or more – underneath a battlemented parapet and set within a walled enclosure, the barmkin. The tower houses of the Lake Counties are part of the two chains of such buildings erected on each side of the Border in waves of activity corresponding to the fluctuations in friendship between the two kingdoms. The Western March was less densely provided with these houses of refuge than the Middle and Eastern Marches and generally the buildings are less substantial and less architecturally elaborate than those of the Scottish Marches. Most tower houses have been

5. Tower house –
Brackenhill, Longtown,
Cumberland

incorporated in later structures, no unaltered barmkin survives,
and, in the absence of excavation, our knowledge of the defensive predecessors of these buildings depends on a few rather
baffling literary references.

Most of the tower houses had a simple rectangular plan without projections. They were three storeys in height; the ground
floor was set under a low segmental barrel vault lit only by one
or two narrow slits widely splayed to the interior. In some
examples it was inaccessible except by a stone spiral staircase
descending from the first floor; most examples have direct access
to the ground floor and it is possible that horses or even cattle
could have been accommodated as suggested by Pennant and
Gilpin, and yet the very restricted space left within the thick
walls would hardly have been adequate for the stock carried by
a family wealthy enough to own a stone tower. Some examples,
especially the later ones, had a conventional timber floor rather
than a stone vault over the lower floor, but a fireproof ground
floor would be essential for effective defence. Entrance to the
first floor was usually by means of an external ladder or a stone
staircase to first floor level, where a heavy oak door was further
protected by a hinged iron grille such as the one which survives
at Naworth Castle or which may be seen at the refuge tower of

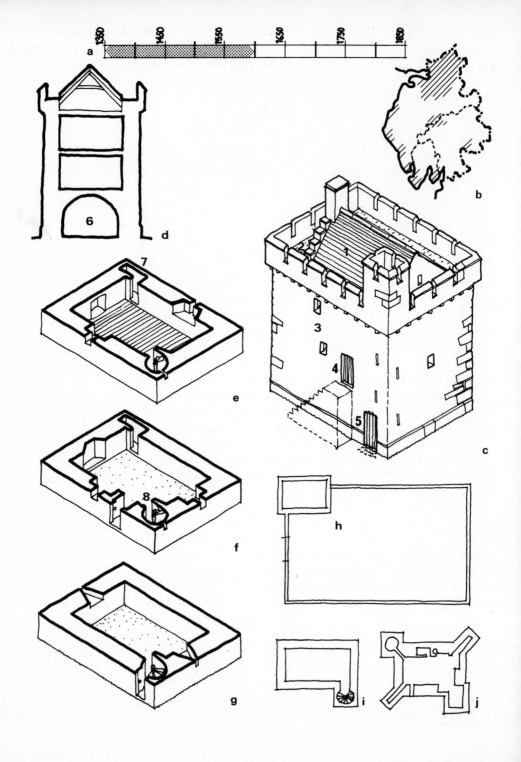

Great Salkeld Parish Church (C). The first floor contained the principal living room or hall with a wall fireplace and small square windows. Above was the chamber or private room, sometimes also with a fireplace. On the top of the building was a walkway behind battlements corbelled out from the wall face and surrounding a roof which was usually gabled and steeply pitched but which was occasionally a lead flat. Sometimes there was a lookout tower raised above one corner and several towers display in addition martial figures standing clear against the skyline, or stone gargoyles masquerading as cannon. The various levels were connected by a stone spiral staircase set within one corner of the building and projecting into the room at each level. In the opposite corner a garderobe was sometimes provided at the end of a mural corridor.

The tower house was normally located at one corner of its barmkin or defensive enclosure, whose high walls were made of stone in the superior examples but possibly of earth or clay, or timber paling protected by clay, in the remainder. Though terms were used rather loosely in contemporary accounts the word pele is consistent with the barmkin rather than the house. The early 19C brick-walled enclosure to the tower at Kirkandrews on Esk (C) may be a reconstruction of just such a barmkin wall.

To judge from 16C accounts of border raiding, the master of the house, being warned of approaching raiders, would drive his stock into the barmkin enclosure, then shut up his family and tenants behind the door and iron grille of his tower house, waiting for the raiders to leave in search of a less well-protected prey or for help to arrive. Defence, therefore, was largely passive and intended to counter lightly armed raiders rather

---

6. Tower houses
a. time scale showing period of construction from about 1350 to about 1600
b. diagram showing areas of greatest concentration; there are scattered examples elsewhere in the region
c. sketch showing pitched roof (1), wall walk (2), small windows (3), first-floor entrance (4), alternative ground-floor entrance (5)
d. cross-section showing vaulted ground floor (6) with two rooms and a garret storey above
e. upper floor with garderobe (7) for chamber
f. intermediate floor acting as hall with spiral staircase (8)
g. ground floor with slit windows
h. tower in relation to walled barmkin which contained barn, stable, and additional domestic quarters
i. alternative plan with projecting staircase wing as at Johnby Hall (C)
j. alternative plan on a larger scale as at Dacre Castle (C)

than armies properly equipped for a siege. Attack depended upon surprise or the use of fire to burn down the door or smoke out the defenders. The accounts suggest that the barmkin contained other buildings – farm buildings, service buildings such as kitchen or brew house, and possibly a more spacious hall for use during the long periods of comparative peace. No doubt these were of timber or some less substantial material.

7. Bastle house – Glassonby, Cumberland

Bastle houses

Although long recognised as a distinct building type the bastle house has only recently received attention comparable to that devoted to tower houses. The term, still unfamiliar, refers to a two-storey elongated defensive dwelling, including provision for refuge for animals as well as their owners and acting as a smaller

8. Bastle houses
a. time scale showing period of construction from about 1540 to 1640
b. map showing concentration of bastle houses near the Border
c. sketch showing ground-floor entrance to cow-house, external stair leading to first-floor entrance to domestic quarters, small barred windows, windows to garret space (example based on Town Head, Newbiggin, Cumrew, C)
d. cross-sections showing normal timber intermediate floor (1) and alternative stone vaulted floor (2)
e. first-floor plan showing larger room which has gable (3) or side wall fireplace (4) and door through partition to smaller, usually unheated room
f. ground-floor plan with space for cattle or horses
g. alternative (and more common) gable entrance to ground floor
h. unglazed window protected by interlaced wrought iron bars

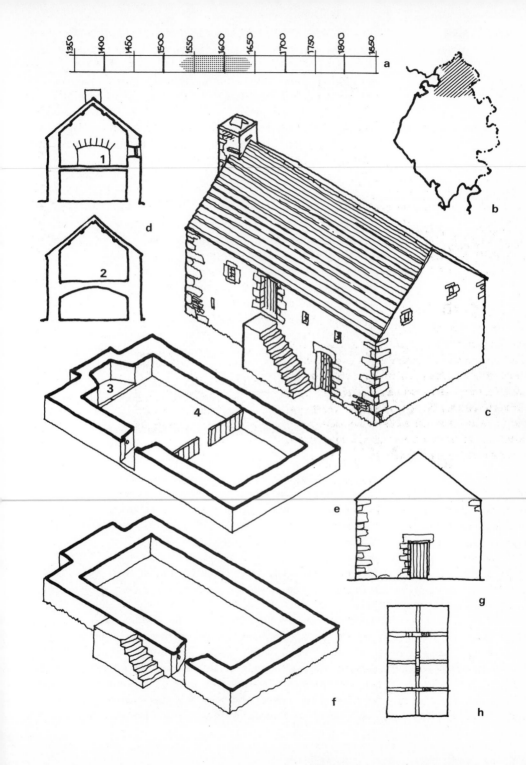

a

b

c

d

1

2

3

4

e

f

g

h

substitute for a tower house and barmkin. In the Lake Counties, examples are confined to the extreme north-east of Cumberland, where they are numerous but only as an extension of a broad band of such dwellings running through Northumberland between 10 and 20 miles south of the Border. Earlier examples may exist but the main period of activity in building bastle houses was the 16C, when lawless clans from both sides of the border used national disputes as a cover for raids on their neighbours of both nationalities.

The living accommodation in a bastle house consisted of two rooms at first floor level. Entrance was from an external ladder or stone staircase into a door about halfway along one of the side walls and so into the larger room. This contained the principal or only fireplace, set into a gable wall usually, though occasionally, in the large bastles, into a side wall; the room was lit by small narrow window openings protected by iron bars. The smaller room opened off the larger and was usually unheated, serving, presumably, as the principal bedroom. Most surviving examples have alterations in the roof but it seems likely that there was a loft or garret at least over the smaller room. The ground floor of a bastle house provided space for cattle and horses, entrance being either from the side wall or through the middle of the gable wall; some light and ventilation came from narrow slit windows. The intermediate floor was usually of wood rather than a stone vault and the surviving examples indicate that there was no internal access between one level and the other.

Defence of a bastle house was purely passive. The simple pitched roof allowed no provision for battlements or a walkway for defenders. One can only assume that at the approach of raiders the animals would be shut into the ground floor. One man would stay with them and close the drawbar; the remainder of the household would shelter in the first floor, ladder drawn up and door secured, all depending on stone walls four feet thick for protection. Clearly the bastle house was a less reliable refuge than the tower house; the determined attacker could batter down the lower door and burn out the defenders above the wooden floor. On the other hand the smaller number of beasts and the presumably less valuable lives would make a bastle house less of a prize for rustling or ransom. In any case border raiding by small bands of thieves was countered by mutual protection of local families who were quite prepared for revenge attacks on the towers and bastles of their adversaries.

No complete example survives; some are ruined, some converted to other uses, some have been incorporated in the walls of later houses or farm buildings; only the unusually rough and heavy masonry or the blocked remains of small splayed window jambs may indicate the former use. Otherwise the name 'stone-house' attached to a modern farm or read in documents may be the only indication of the architectural response to the social conditions of the 16C.

The tower houses and bastle houses, being refuges as much as dwellings, retained and modified archaic forms because of special local conditions. At the same time, during lulls in border conflict, and in districts remote from danger, the design of Large Houses in the Lake Counties reflected the national development of the house based on an open hall both in the T-shaped and H-shaped versions.

Semi-fortified houses

The T-shaped house had a two-storey wing at right angles to the open hall; the wing usually contained a private apartment or solar (itself open to the roof) on the upper floor and service rooms below; the hall, open to the roof and initially heated by an open hearth, was a more public room; the two were linked by a cross-passage at the junction between hall and wing. An outside kitchen, barn, stable, and other farm buildings completed the building group and all were enclosed within a wall and gate-house, or, exceptionally in the Lake Counties, occupied a moated site. Most local examples of the T-shaped house have lost their identity through later alterations, but Kirkby Thore Hall (W) still retains the essentials of the plan, and other extended tower houses, such as Ormside Hall and Asby Rectory (W) show a clear affinity to the plan.

The H-shaped house consisted of a central open hall flanked by two-storey wings, one of which contained private apart-ments, and the other chambers or bedrooms over service rooms. The open hall originally had a central hearth but this was re-placed by a fireplace in the centre of one of the side walls in the more important houses and backing on to the cross-passage in the lesser examples. Doors led from the cross-passage into the buttery and pantry of the service wing and into a passage between the two which led to the outside kitchen. At the oppo-site end of the hall there was access to a parlour or dining room and to stairs rising to the solar. The upper floors at each end were quite independent and, at the lower end especially, might alternatively be reached by an external staircase. Again, the house, kitchen and farm buildings formed a group which usually had some enclosing wall or ditch.

9. Semi-fortified house – Yanwath Hall, Westmorland

While draughty and uncomfortable by modern standards, such houses, even in the poor and remote northern counties, were more than simply utilitarian. Windows, especially at the upper end of the house, had moulded mullions and transoms and traceried heads; arch-braced collar beam roof trusses exposed to the open halls were moulded and cusped, and some of the rooms would be enlivened by wainscotting and hangings.

Examples of such houses, though found throughout the Lake Counties, are most common in the Eden Valley and in the south, around Kendal. Within the vernacular zone they include Beetham and Middleton Halls (W), both retaining sections of enclosing wall, and Preston Patrick Hall (W), which has

10. Semi-fortified and other hall houses
a. time scale showing period of construction from about 1400 to 1600
b. map showing examples distributed throughout the region
c. sketch (based partly on Yanwath Hall, W) showing a house with a central hall, the upper wing carried up as a defensible tower (1) and the lower wing a kitchen which also could be made into a tower (2)
d. cross section showing hall open to the roof
e. ground-floor plan with vaulted cellar and solar above (3), hall (4), fireplace backing on to cross-passage (5), kitchen (6)
f. alternative ground-floor plan showing fireplace in side wall (7), cross-passage (8), buttery (9), pantry (10), passage to outside kitchen (11); these last three usually have stone vaults above
g. diagrammatic arrangement (based on Burneside Hall, W) showing semi-fortified house (12), kitchen garth (13), walled yard (14), gate-house (15)
h. T-shaped hall house (based on Kirkby Thore Hall, W)
i. H-shaped hall house (based on Preston Patrick Hall, W)
j. house with two defensive wings (based on Howgill Castle, W)

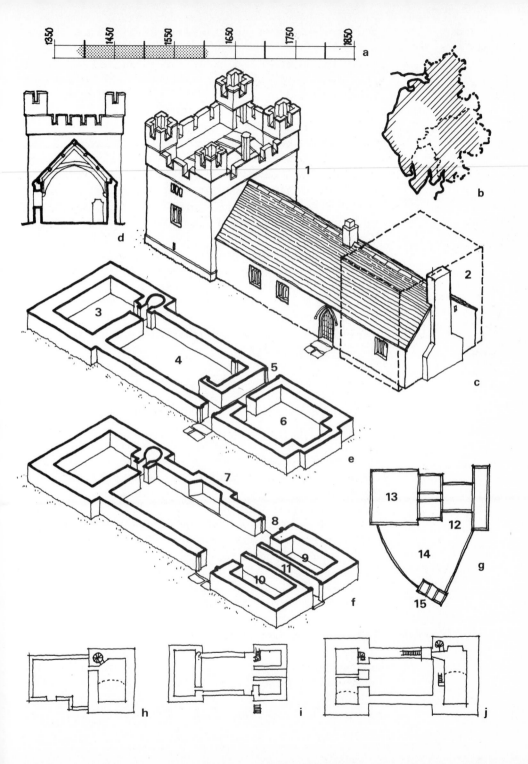

a

1350 1450 1550 1650 1750 1850

b

d

1

2

c

3
4
5
6

e

7
8
9
10 11

f

13
12
14
15

g

h

i

j

windows designed for shutters and drawbar rather than glazing, and a first-floor Court Room with external staircase access. There are several others, such as Wharton Hall (W), which were so extensive, or belonged to such important families, that, in the context of the poverty-stricken Lake Counties, they must be admitted as outside the vernacular zone.

Many of the medieval Large Houses, being subject to raids from directly across the Border or indirectly by way of the coast or the mountains, included some provision for occasional defence or refuge. This was met by light fortification of the whole structure, like the bastle houses, or, more commonly, by taking up one part as a tower providing a refuge or strong point, much as the keep or gatehouse of a medieval castle could be held even if all else were lost.

Several towers were attached to domestic buildings which have disappeared entirely, as at Clifton (W), or Ulpha (C), or have been replaced by later buildings, as at Catterlen (C) or Kentmere (W). It is possible that there were formerly timber-framed domestic buildings attached to the stone towers. The mid-16C survey of defensible dwellings in the Middle Marches of Northumberland refers to tower and attached stonehouse as if they were considered separately and with the implication that a stonehouse was something unusual, and so it might have been on the Western Marches. Even so early and well-preserved a house as Yanwath Hall (W) has a tower of separate build from its hall.

In many examples, however, one part of the house, usually the upper end, has been taken up as a tower. In arrangement such a tower resembles a self-contained tower-house with its walls four feet or more in thickness, its vaulted ground floor ceiling, its battlemented parapet and watch tower, and its spiral staircase connecting various levels; but the staircase was entered from within the house and at ground floor rather than by way of an external ladder to first floor. Examples include Killington Hall (W).

In some other examples both the upper and the lower cross wing have been raised and battlemented, though usually only one, that at the upper end, was seriously defensible. Blencow Hall (C) is one such example and the late 17C drawings by Machell of Burnside Hall (W) show towers at both ends, though only one, at the north end, had thick walls and a stone vaulted bottom storey. Howgill Castle, Milburn (W), is unique in having truly defensible towers at both ends of the hall, both towers having walls 10 feet thick, heavy stone barrel vaults, and, originally, battlemented parapets since removed. Smardale Hall, Waitby (W), has four rounded turrets, one at each corner of the rectangular building, giving a military appearance though without defensive thickness.

These semi-defensive dwellings are difficult to date. Most of them have some mouldings or tracery for which an approximate date may be suggested on national evidence, but the time lag between this and other less remote districts and the unpretentious size and quality of the houses of families locally important makes accurate comparison very difficult or unreliable. The houses appear to have been erected in two phases, in the 14C and in the late 15C and the 16C. Their distribution presumably corresponds with the distribution of population here in the Middle Ages, but they cluster between Carlisle and Bewcastle in the north, around Penrith in the east, and around the River Kent in the south. They are to be found scattered along the Pennine slopes, where raiders could travel through the waste lands to descend on the valley, and also on inlets from the Cumberland coast, where raids could be mounted from the sea. Although from time to time considered as part of a national defensive system against the Scots they were really personal or local refuges, the great castles at Carlisle, Brougham, Appleby, Egremont, Kendal, etc., providing real defence for the kingdom,

The desire for increased comfort and privacy led to a general change from designs based on the hall open to the roof and heated by an open fire to those based on a building two or three storeys throughout and heated by several fires in conventional wall fireplaces. These changes may be observed in the Large Houses built in the Lake Counties during the 16C and early 17C.

Later non-fortified houses – without an open hall

In a typical house of this period the H-plan of central block and cross wings was preserved but the hall became a single storey room, heated from a fireplace and serving as a living room or unheated and serving as a circulation space; off the hall one cross wing included parlour and dining room, the other cross wing comprised a set of kitchen, scullery, and other service rooms now added to the houses rather than found in detached impermanent buildings. Above, there were bedrooms, corresponding to the rooms below, one opening off another. Access was usually by way of a stone staircase in a projecting wing, but otherwise no more convenient or ostentatious than the narrow spiral stair of a fortified house. Entrance might be through a vestigial through passage but there was a tendency to place the entrance in the centre of the main elevation with

11. Non-fortified house –
Hincaster Hall,
Westmorland

windows placed symmetrically on each side, false windows
maintaining a balance where required by the plan.

During this period panelled walls and plastered ceilings
helped to improve comfort, and there were crude imitations on
ceiling or frieze of the fine plasterwork to be seen in more important houses like Levens Hall or Calgarth Hall, complete with
classical allusions and patriotic emblems. As windows increased
in number and size so the use of glass became more general and
provision for defence and refuge became less. The transition
from narrow medieval houses to deep houses of Renaissance
inspiration was about to take place.

12. Later non-fortified houses – without an open hall
a. time scale showing period of use from about 1560 to 1700
b. map showing examples found throughout the region
c. isometric (based mainly on Newby Hall, W) showing many windows
and projecting wings
d. cross-section showing two storeys, chamber over hall, and space for
garrets above
e. first-floor plan showing bedrooms (1, 2, 3)
f. ground-floor plan with hall (4), parlour (5), kitchen (6), staircase in a
projecting wing (7), an alternative, central, position for doorway
shown
g. alternative plan (based partly on Collinfield, Kendal, W) with hall
(8), kitchen (9) in a projecting wing
h. alternative plan (based on Barwise Hall, W) with hall (10), parlour
(11), kitchen (12) and later staircase projection (13)
i. alternative plan (based on Kirkby Hall, Kirkby Ireleth, L, after
H. S. Cowper) with hall (14), parlour (15), kitchen (16)

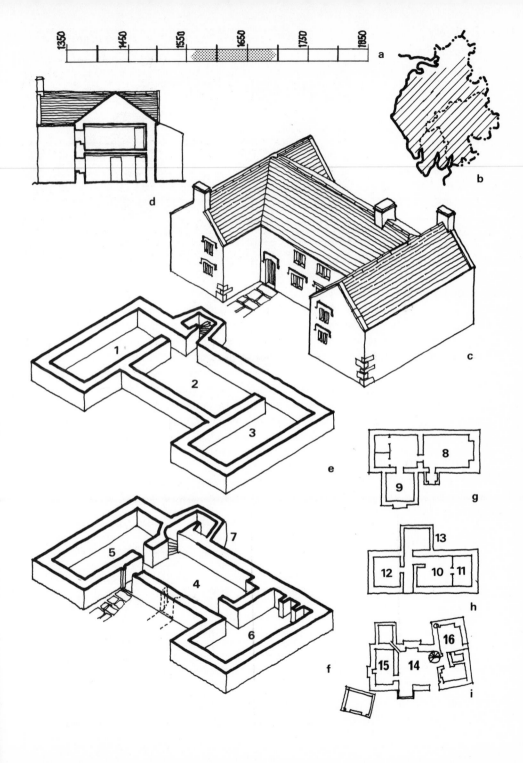

a

b

c

d

e
1
2
3

f
5
7
4
6

g
8
9

h
13
12
10 11

i
16
15 14

13. Multi-storey porch
house – Gaythorn Hall,
Asby, Westmorland

Multi-storey porch houses

There was, however, in the Lake Counties, as elsewhere in the north of England, a brief period in which simple non-fortified houses were equipped with a multi-storey porch giving emphasis to the entrance, and, perhaps, acknowledging the former importance of gatehouse and tower. Lacking any open hall or other room open to the roof their construction lacks the interest of some of their predecessors, but with large mullioned and transomed windows, elaborate doorways, and stress on coats of arms or other carven devices the multi-storey porches bring grace and decorative interest to a building type in which solidity and a forbidding aspect had formerly been the predominant characteristics.

Examples of this type had a living room equivalent to the hall but with a wooden or plaster ceiling, a parlour, withdrawing

14. Houses with a multi-storey porch
a. time scale showing period of use from about 1580 to 1700
b. map showing widespread location of examples
c. sketch (based partly on Greenthwaite Hall, C) showing three-storey porch rising above main eaves (1)
d. cross section showing two full storeys and a garret space formed with the aid of upper crucks (2)
e. first-floor plan showing fireplaces to several chambers
f. ground-floor plan with hall (3), parlour (4), kitchen (5) and porch with open doorway and incorporating spiral staircase (6)
g. alternative plan (based partly on Hornby Hall, W) with hall (7), parlour (8), kitchen (9), porch (10)
h. alternative plan with projecting porches and staircase wings as at Gaythorn Hall (W) and Hesket Hall (C)

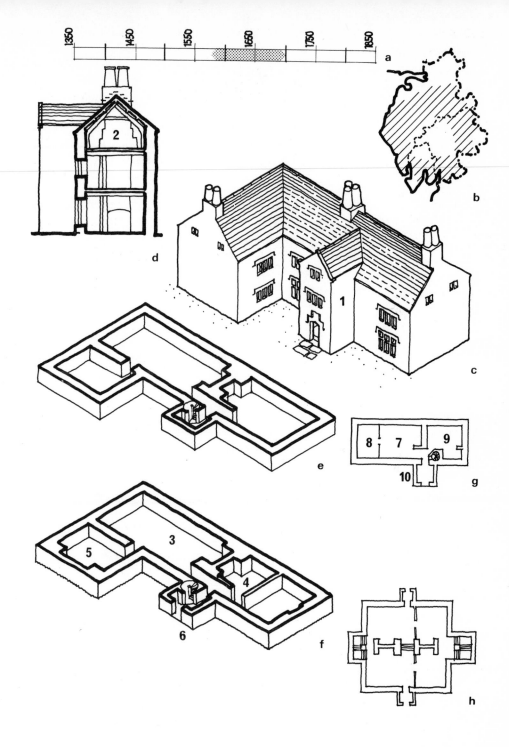

Large Houses

Renaissance influence

room or dining room, and a kitchen and other service rooms on the ground floor, chambers on the first floor and garrets above. A narrow stone spiral staircase rose from floor to floor and was sometimes incorporated in the multi-storey porch. This projected from the middle of the main elevation and had an open doorway at ground floor level, a small room above, often called on slender evidence a chapel, and a further tiny room within the gabled roof space. Such a porch was the counterpart in stone to the elaborately decorated porches of timber frame houses like Little Moreton Hall in Cheshire.

Among the houses with these characteristics may be mentioned Greenthwaite Hall, and Millrigg, Culgaith, in Cumberland; Hornby Hall, Brougham and Kirkbarrow, Barton, in Westmorland. All these houses are one room in depth but a few examples, of which Gaythorn Hall, Asby (W) and Hesket Hall (C) are the chief, are compact, almost cubic houses, two rooms in depth, and with wide projecting staircase wings at the gables to balance the multi-storey porches at front and back. Gaythorn Hall is especially interesting for its staircases of solid baulks of timber winding in separate flights around a solid timber core and for the duplication of rooms and features which has led to the suggestion that it might have been designed for the occupation of two families.

Large Houses under Renaissance influence

The Large Houses of the Lake Counties were designed according to Renaissance precedent from the last few years of the 17C until, in the early part of the 19C, they passed as Gothic Revival houses over the Polite Threshold and out of the Vernacular Zone. There were three main phases: a robust Anglo-Baroque, a more refined Georgian and a more affected Regency and Revival phase.

Anglo-baroque

The typical house of the first phase was a double-pile house, i.e., two rooms in depth, with a symmetrical front elevation, and two storeys in height but with garrets above. On the ground floor were hall/living room, parlour, kitchen, dairy, etc., and there were bedrooms above, including the servants' rooms and storage space in the garrets. Linking the different floors there was a spacious framed wooden staircase, rising in short flights around an open well, with turned balusters and decorated newels, and placed to be seen rather than hidden in a corner. The rooms were much taller than previously, adding height in elevation to the compactness of plan. Externally there were rows of tall windows symmetrically disposed about a carefully emphasised entrance, the windows originally having a stone mullion and transom

44

and side hung casement opening lights (though in most cases vertically sliding sashes have been inserted as replacement) and the doorway having boldly projecting bolection moulds and probably a broken pediment above. The elevation was divided by string courses and contained within projecting or other rusticated quoins. At the sides and rear, mullioned windows of archaic pattern remained in use, and generally the occasional obsolete details or the crude or incorrect treatment of classical details confirmed the ignorance on which the boldness was really based.

Houses of Anglo-baroque character, appearing at the same time in many parts of the country, and influenced by such famous designs as that of Sir Roger Pratt for Coleshill in Berkshire, must have amazed the countryside by their symmetry, their regular composition, and the foreign character of their ornament. Examples in the Lake Counties include Mansion House, Eamontbridge in Westmorland.

Georgian

The reversion from the robust Anglo-baroque of Wren and Hawksmoor with its French and Dutch inspiration to the stricter classicism of Burlington and Campbell which took place nationally from about 1720 may be seen in the Lake Counties only slightly later. The Large Houses built from about 1740 to about 1800 show the influence of the Palladian movement among British architects, percolating no doubt through the medium of pattern books to this part of rural Britain.

45

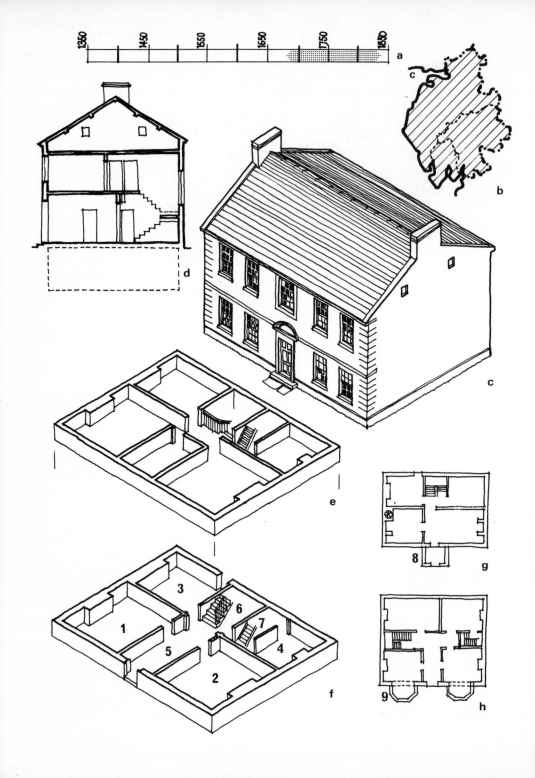

a

b

c

c

d

e

f

1

2

3

4

5

6

7

g

8

h

9

Plan forms changed little from the Anglo-baroque phase. Most such houses were two rooms in depth, rooms being disposed on each side of a central hall or lobby which led from the front door to a prominent and well-lit staircase at the rear, and most were two storeys in height, though three storey houses were becoming more common. In general organisation elevations changed little either, windows being placed symmetrically about a central doorway, but proportions more crude than correct in the earlier phase become academically acceptable in the later and details ill-conceived or misunderstood become carefully designed and well executed. At the vernacular level designers and craftsmen could learn from the Great Houses erected to the

16. Anglo-baroque, Georgian, and Regency houses
a. time scale showing period of use from about 1680 to 1840
b. map showing distribution widespread throughout the region
c. sketch based partly on Hall Farm, Ousby (C) showing symmetry, use of two main storeys and two rooms' depth under one roof
d. cross-section showing basement, two principal floors and attics
e. first floor plan showing four bedrooms, all with fireplaces, main staircase, and service stair rising to attics
f. ground-floor plan with living room (1), parlour (2), kitchen (3), scullery (4), lobby (5), main staircase (6) and service stair (7). There were often additional outbuildings forming wings and extensions to the main block
g. earlier alternative plan (based on Mansion House, Eamontbridge, W) showing single storey porch (8)
h. alternative plan with side wall staircase and bay windows (9)

47

18. Large House with
Greek Revival details –
Easton, Bowness,
Cumberland

designs of professional architects, such as Carr of York or
Webster of Kendal who were working in the Lake Counties, as
well as profiting from the pattern books which were freely
circulating and so available to every master builder or brick-
layer. Large Houses of the Georgian phase, on the fringe of the
Vernacular Zone, may be found in all parts of the region but they
are most common in the Eden Valley and the West Cumberland
coastlands where agriculture prospered in the second half of the
18C, and sandstone was available and suitable for the precise
mouldings and smooth wall surfaces of these reticent but
graceful houses.

Regency and Revival

By 1800 the Large Houses had all but passed out of the vernacular zone and displayed few vernacular qualities. Some little local
character persisted among the attenuated proportions and the
Grecian details of the Regency and Greek Revival phases or in
the examples of Gothic Revival taste which were erected in a
region which had barely forgotten Gothic architecture itself.

Plan forms showed little substantial change from previous
phases though deep projecting bay or bow windows broke up the
clean lines of the plans and open columnar porches, balconies
and verandahs enhanced plain stucco elevations. Roofs, low-
pitched, hipped and increasingly of Welsh slates, hid behind
cornice and blocking course. Details showing Italian, Greek or
Gothic influence were obviously due to national influences of
taste, though some buildings like the White House, Appleby,
display local inventiveness.

The various plan types have been separately described and examples survive with little external alteration to represent the various phases, but many houses bear the marks of the alterations and extensions of successive owners and some Large Houses have been so enlarged that their original features are submerged in later Great Houses. At the same time, as Large Houses pass out of the vernacular zone they are represented by late and small examples little bigger than large farmhouses.

Conclusion

Small Houses

In the Lake Counties, the Small Houses, those designed for the occupation of yeomen, tenant farmers, minor clergymen, millers, etc., emerge fully developed in permanent materials about the middle of the 17C and were within the vernacular zone, through various changes of plan, until the second half of the 19C.

In our present state of knowledge of vernacular architecture it is quite impossible to picture with any accuracy the sort of Small House built in the district before the middle 17C. Nevertheless, the relatively *developed* plan forms which emerged suggest that the change of building material rather than the change of plan was the more important. This being so one would expect the 16C and early 17C Small House at least to be a miniature hall house, one room, heated by an open hearth or gable fireplace and open to the roof, off which opened another, smaller room, which possibly had a loft over. Over the whole area, but especially in the southern part of the Lake District, this 'hall and bower' would be the dwelling house. In the northern Lake District, the Solway Plain and the Eden Valley, the two-unit house would be attached by way of a cross-passage to a third domestic 'service' unit, following the precedent of earlier Large Houses, or to an agricultural building as a longhouse. The houses would probably be cruck-framed with enclosing walls of wattle and daub, clay, turf, or roughly piled fieldstones. At the moment one is equally uncertain about the reason for the sudden use of permanent materials and expensive construction including moulded and dated doorways, but the confirmation of tenants in their customary tenure with right of inheritance by a decision of the King's Bench in 1625 may have encouraged men who were virtually freeholders to invest in property on their own secure lands.

The two-unit plan, the cross-passage and downhouse plan, and the longhouse and its derivatives will be considered separately, though, whatever may have been their separate origins, all three plans were in use simultaneously when rebuilding occurred during the 17C.

19. Two-unit house – Pelutho, Holme St. Cuthbert, Cumberland (this house had clay walls with stone dressings and formerly had a thatched roof)

The two-unit house

The heart of the two-unit house was the general living room, variously called the house, the fire-house, the kitchen, etc. This room contained the principal or only hearth and was the place in which cooking, eating, and general domestic tasks and crafts were conducted. Off this living room opened a second, smaller room, the parlour or bower, which was the principal bedroom, and which in the later and superior examples had a small fireplace built against the wall. Part of the parlour was often partitioned off as a buttery or dairy with its own door to the living room. Over these rooms there was a continuous loft which was originally contained almost entirely in the roof space but which gradually was given taller side walls until it become a full height room and was divided into separate chambers or bedrooms. In early and inferior examples the loft was reached by a steep ladder/staircase but later a stone spiral staircase rising from the bower or a stone staircase housed in a projecting bulge at the rear of the living room was used. Only in late and superior Small Houses was there any fireplace on the upper floor.

The principal fire of wood, peat, or, where available, outcrop coal was made on a hearth stone set against one gable wall and forming the base of an inglenook. Above, there was a hooded chimney, consisting of a wide flue gathered together in a hollow half-pyramid to join the chimney stack. The hooded chimney was made of studs lined with wattle, clay daub and plaster, and joined a stone chimney stack which was carried on wooden cantilevered beams. In later examples both chimney and stack were made of stone, retaining the original shape but in a graceful curve. At one side of the hearth there was a stone or timber

51

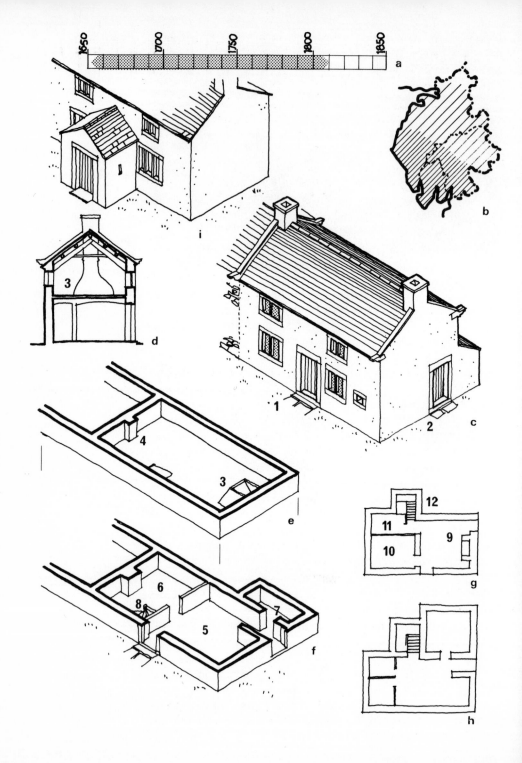

1650 1700 1750 1800 1850 a

b

c

1

2

d

3

e

3

4

f

5

6

7

8

g

9

10

11

12

h

i

partition called the 'heck' and this shielded the inglenook from the worst of the draughts from the door. At the other side the front wall of the house included a small window, the 'fire window' which lit the deep inglenook. The hearth wall usually included a recess which served as a salt or 'spice cupboard' and other recesses or 'keeping holes' presumably for a lamp, fire-side implements, etc. Windows were confined to the front wall except for a small window or ventilator serving the buttery at the rear. The doorway was originally in the gable wall leading into the short passage formed by the heck partition, but there was an increasing tendency for a 'front' door to be placed near the middle of the main elevation and opening straight into the living room; the gable door thus became a 'back' door.

The basic plan had several variations; e.g., a projecting wing or turret at the rear enclosed a staircase, a lean-to extension at the rear served as a back-kitchen, scullery, or brew-house, or a full gabled wing at the rear contained a separate kitchen and a chamber above; but the plan was in use in its essentials for Small Houses from the middle of the 17C until the early 19C and then its elements were adapted for use as one of the Cottage plans.

Cross-passage and downhouse plan

The 'cross-passage and downhouse' plan consisted, like the two-unit plan, of two main living rooms on the ground floor, but in addition there was a substantial service room at one end. A cross-passage ran from the front to the back of the house alongside the wall containing the principal or only hearth; in effect it was outside the house proper, and indeed is sometimes called an 'outside cross-passage' because access to the house

20. Two-unit houses
a. time scale showing period of use from about 1650 to 1810
b. map showing widespread use with concentration in south
c. sketch based partly on a house at Yearngill (C) showing house one room in depth; entrance may be on front (1) or on gable (2)
d. cross section showing loft or bedroom space with firehood rising up gable wall (3)
e. first floor plan with firehood (3) at 'lower' end and applied chimney breast (4) at 'upper' end
f. ground floor plan with living room (5), parlour/bedroom (6), pantry (7), stone spiral staircase (8)
g. alternative plan (based partly on Under Howe, Grasmere, W) with living room (9), parlour (10), pantry (11), staircase (12)
h. alternative plan showing a wing serving as a dairy or, if with a fire-place, either as a kitchen or an additional parlour
i. alternative sketch showing the single-storey porch which was some-times added, sometimes incorporated in the original construction

Cross-passage and
downhouse plan

21. House with cross-
passage and downhouse
– Cotehill, Cumberland
(the external staircase
appears to lead to a
granary over the down-
house)

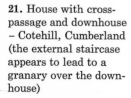

was through a doorway in the hearth wall near the end of the
cross-passage and by way of the short lobby formed by the 'heck'
partition, just as if one were coming into a two-unit house from
the open air. The cross-passage ran through the 'downhouse' or
service room. Normally unheated, the downhouse apparently
acted as a scullery, an implement store, a fuel store, and a
brewhouse; in early and small examples it was open to the roof,
but in later examples it was lofted to provide a granary or a
chamber above, and the cross-passage was defined by a timber

22. Cross-passage houses with downhouse
a. time scale showing period of construction from about 1660 to 1820
b. map showing concentration in the northern half of the region
c. composite sketch showing position of door (1) in relation to chimney
   stack (2) and fire window (3)
d. cross-section showing outshut containing staircase and pantry (4),
   upper floor in roof space (5) with upper crucks (6)
e. first floor plan showing loft space (7) and downhouse open to the roof
   (8)
f. ground floor plan with living room (9), parlour (10), pantry (11),
   staircase (12), cross-passage or 'hallan' (13), downhouse (14)
g. alternative plan (based on a house in Cumrew, C) showing spiral
   staircase rising to the loft from the parlour (15)
h. alternative plan showing a fireplace in the parlour (16) and a fireplace with oven making the downhouse a kitchen (17)
i. alternative plan showing the parlour with its fireplace in the position
   of the downhouse (18) and the staircase in a bulge from the rear wall
   (19)

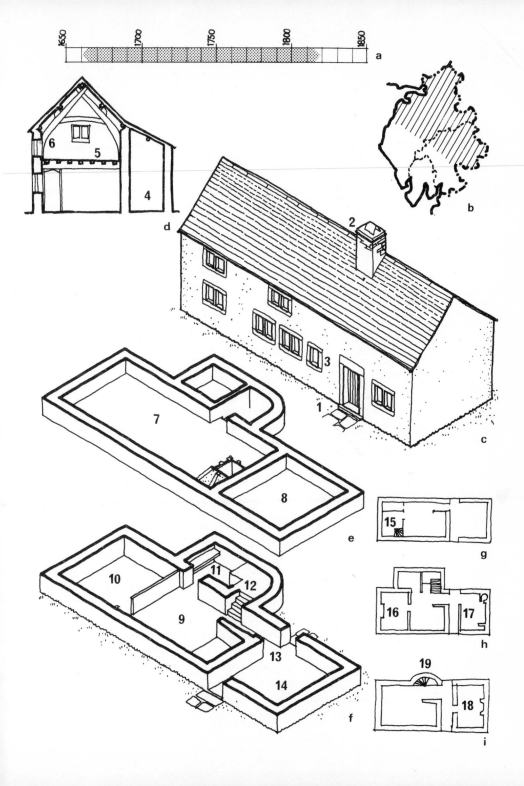

a

b

c

d

e

f

g

h

i

1 2 3 4 5 6 7 8 9 10 11 12 13 14 15 16 17 18 19

1650 1700 1750 1800 1850

partition or by a wall. Eventually it was provided with a fire-place and was made into a kitchen in the modern sense, taking most of the cooking, feed preparation and water heating, all messy activities, out of the general living room. Usually the front door to the cross-passage was the front door to the house and was given the arched head, moulded jambs or decorated lintel which testified to its importance; but the fashion for a symmetrical elevation became so strong that another door was eventually inserted, to lead directly into the living room; a more fashionable approach to the house no doubt, but, except where there was a porch, less satisfactory for the comfort of the in-habitants.

It was, of course, possible to convert a two-unit house into one with a cross-passage by adding a wing at one end, but in most cases the continuous roof, the absence of any straight joint on the front wall, and the continuity of architectural detail, show that all was of one build. Furthermore, in not one example investigated did the door leading from the cross-passage into the living room bear any indication by moulding, decoration, or even by dressed stones at the jamb that it had been an outside doorway; the signs were to the contrary.

Houses of this plan might have staircase projections, out-shuts, and projecting wings like those of two-unit houses. They were in use throughout the northern half of the Lake Counties from the middle of the 17C to the last few years of the 18C, and, indeed, examples which appear from the exterior to have the characteristics of the plan have been found with dates as late as 1823.

Houses with cross-passage and attached farm buildings

The true longhouse is an elongated building which contains accommodation for men and animals at opposite ends of the one building, erected at one time, under one roof, with intercom-munication between the two, and with entrance into the dwel-ling house by way of the farm buildings. Few such houses survive intact anywhere, but there are in the Lake Counties, and especially in the northern and eastern parts, many houses which have characteristics obviously derived from the long-house.

The basic accommodation in such a house is similar to that of the two-unit house: a living room, a parlour, and a buttery on the ground floor, a loft above, a fireplace or hearth in the end wall of the living room. The method of entry by way of a cross-passage *outside* the domestic accommodation is that of the cross-passage and downhouse plan, but in place of a domestic service

room there are farm buildings. These may consist only of a cow-house with a loft above or they may include cow-house, barn, and stable; they may be of the same height, rather lower, or even taller than the domestic buildings (alterations to both agricultural and domestic sections obscure the original arrangement); they may retain intercommunication with the domestic quarters, the doors may have been blocked, or such intercommunication may once have been possible and lost in later improvements. The cattle may once have reached their stalls through the common cross-passage but no surviving example with this arrangement has been discovered in the region.

It is doubtful whether the convenience of direct undercover access from hearth to cattle was regarded as any great benefit by the 17C or 18C farmer; most farms, including those built in later times when comfort was a greater consideration, and those built in the coldest and wettest parts of the region, lacked any such convenience. However, adequate accommodation of cattle, especially oxen, was very important when they provided the plough teams and when they were the chief draught animals in a mixed farming economy, and intercommunication would certainly be no handicap, rather would lead to supervision and security. The association of a farming family and its cattle is an ancient one; there are traditions of the importance of allowing the cattle to see the fire, there are even traditions that the heat and smell of the cattle was at one time considered a benefit rather than the opposite. Above all there is the widespread use

23. Cross-passage house with attached farm buildings – Little Bampton, Cumberland (there is a straight joint suggesting that a loft has been raised over the cow-house which also has a separate door and an inserted window)

57

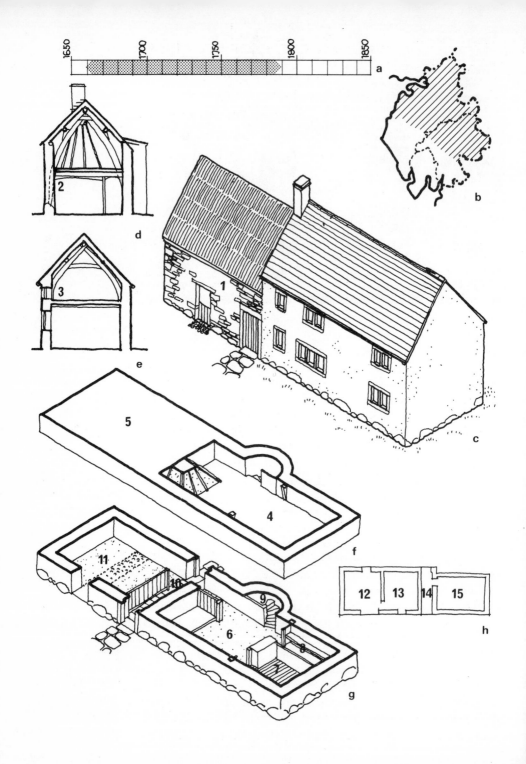

of the basic longhouse plan which recent excavation of medieval sites has shown was predominant in England generally, and which local excavation has shown was found among the predecessors of these 17C houses in the Lake Counties.

Houses of the cross-passage plan with attached farm buildings continued to be built until late in the 18C. As in the other plan types described there was a tendency for another front door to be added to the middle of the main elevation of the domestic part, but this was by no means universal. Houses in which the cross-passage door was the only front door, and was given the decoration appropriate to its status, were built as late as 1774. However, study of buildings of this plan is complicated by the practice, which may have been longstanding, of alternate rebuilding, i.e., of rebuilding the domestic and agricultural portions of a longhouse at different times, rather like the alternate rebuilding of nave and chancel in a parish church. It is possible that on an ancient longhouse site the domestic buildings were re-erected in permanent materials first and the farmbuildings later, perhaps not until the later 18C or even the 19C. Then the nature and extent of the farmbuildings would be hidden except where a plinth of heavy boulders cleared from the fields and serving as a base for the superstructure gives some indication of the dimensions of the earlier buildings.

The upper floor of a two-unit plan house changed its role from storage loft to bedroom as the side walls became higher, as full size windows were introduced into these walls, as headroom

Outshut plans

24. Cross-passage house with farm buildings
a. time scale showing period of erection from about 1660 to 1790
b. map showing concentration in northern half of the region
c. sketch showing position of door in relation to chimney stack and fire window, attached cow-house with low eaves (1). Although the house is shown to the right of the cross-passage it could equally be to the left with farm buildings to the right
d. cross-section with access by mural staircase to loft at first floor, and use of full crucks (2)
e. alternative cross-section showing taller loft space and use of upper crucks (3)
f. first-floor plan with loft space used as bedroom (4), and loft over cow-house (5)
g. ground-floor plan with living room (6), parlour (7), pantry (8), mural staircase (9), cross-passage (10), cow-house (11), reached both from the cross-passage and directly from the farmyard
h. alternative plan (based on buildings in Hilton, W) with barn (12), cow house (13) and cross-passage (14) rebuilt alongside an older house (15)

25. Small House with continuous outshut – Floristonrigg, Cumberland (the gable wall shows the roof swept down to cover the outshut)

improved, and as a satisfactory means of access was developed. The ladder or steep companion way staircase gave way to the stone staircase, at first a tight, narrow flight of steps crowded in a mere bulge protruding from the rear wall but later a 'dog leg' staircase of two flights in a substantial projecting turret or wing, and eventually to a wooden newel staircase, properly illuminated and contained in an extension at the rear of the building. In each case the projection was roofed by a continuation of the main roof and was an 'outshut'.

Quite separately there had been a tendency for extra accommodation to be gained on the ground floor of a house to serve as a dairy or scullery, by way of a projection from the rear wall,

26. Continuous outshut houses
a. time scale showing period of use about 1730 to 1820
b. map showing widespread distribution in the region
c. sketch showing outshut covered by a continuation of the main roof (1) and gable entrance (2) or the more common front entrance (3)
d. cross-section showing two-storey height and staircase within the outshut
e. first-floor plan with bedrooms (4, 5, 6), storage space (7) and upper part of scullery (8)
f. ground-floor plan with living room (9), parlour (10), scullery (11), pantry (12) and staircase (13)
g., h., and **i.** show three stages in development of the plan: the originating plan of a two-unit house with a staircase (14) in a projecting 'turret', the developing plan with a stair in three flights and a pantry added to the outshut (15), and the developed plan with a scullery (16) added to make the outshut run continuously along the rear of the house

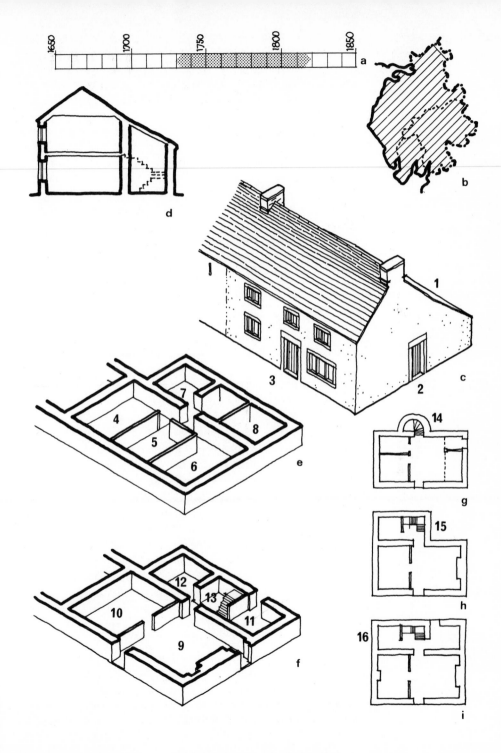

again covered by an extension of the main roof. Such an outshut could be added to an existing house, or could be incorporated in a new build.

The staircase outshut and the service outshut were placed under the same 'catslide' or (locally) 'toofall' continuation of the main roof; with the addition of further rooms the whole rear wall was eventually occupied by a continuous outshut. The building was still conceived as one room in depth, the roof loads were still carried by the original rear wall of the house, the additional rooms and staircase were shallower than the original rooms, and they were usually open to their lean-to roof, but the process of changing to a plan two rooms in depth was well under way.

As the first floor of the house grew taller so the height above the ground floor outshut spaces increased, became wasteful or, over a dairy, perhaps even unhygienic. By lofting over these spaces then low narrow storerooms became available on the upper floor, reached from the landing at the head of the stairs. The side walls of these rooms were increased in height until they could be used as bedrooms, but they were still contained in an extension of the main roof, and the eaves at the rear were substantially lower than the eaves at the front. Externally, apart from the outshut at the rear, such houses were similar to the later versions of the two-unit plan. There was a front door, near the middle of the elevation but rarely at the centre. It was offset in order to give a reasonable balance in the size of the two principal rooms. Windows were equally spaced on each side, there was rarely a fire window as the inglenook and hooded chimney had been superseded by the conventional wall fireplace, there were full height windows on the first floor. The difference in level between the eaves at front and back of the house remained characteristic of the plan type.

It is sometimes difficult without close examination to distinguish between houses built from the first with outshuts and those older houses to which outshuts have been added, especially where there has been a change in roofing material. However, houses built or extended to this plan may be found throughout the Lake Counties and may bear dates between 1730 and 1820.

Double-pile houses

A Small House of double-pile plan has four rooms on each floor: on the ground floor a living room and parlour at the front and back kitchen and dairy at the rear; on the first floor four bedrooms or three bedrooms and a cheese room. Entrance was by way of a front door straight into the living room; there was a

27. Double-pile Small
House – Arkleby,
Plumbland, Cumberland
(two realistic 'blind
windows' may be seen)

back door leading from the back kitchen; the staircase at the
rear rose between back-kitchen and dairy; the whole was contained under one roof of equal pitch, eaves being of similar
height at front and rear. Such a house may be considered as a
logical development from houses one room deep, through addition of outshuts – a development upwards – or it may be considered as a miniature copy of the double-pile Large House built
for the ordinary farmer's social superiors; in either case as a
compact, economical, though spacious plan it was an appropriate culmination to the constantly improving house plans at
the vernacular level.

It needed little further development for the plan with continuous two-storey outshuts at the rear to become the double-
pile plan. The ridge moved to the centre of the house as the
whole came under one roof and the eaves at the rear were raised
to meet the level of the eaves at the front. Partition walls were
made substantial enough to carry purlins and no roof truss was
necessary. Equally it needed little imagination for the local
builder to reduce the dimensions and height of the double-pile
Large House to those appropriate for a farmhouse; the attic
storeys designed for the landlord's servants became the garret
space for his tenant's apples. The plan remained satisfactory
with little modification until Small Houses passed out of the
vernacular zone in the second half of the 19C. One development,
however, was to improve the comfort of the living room by
adding a partition and so forming a lobby or passage between
front door and staircase, lit by a fanlight or glazed panels along-

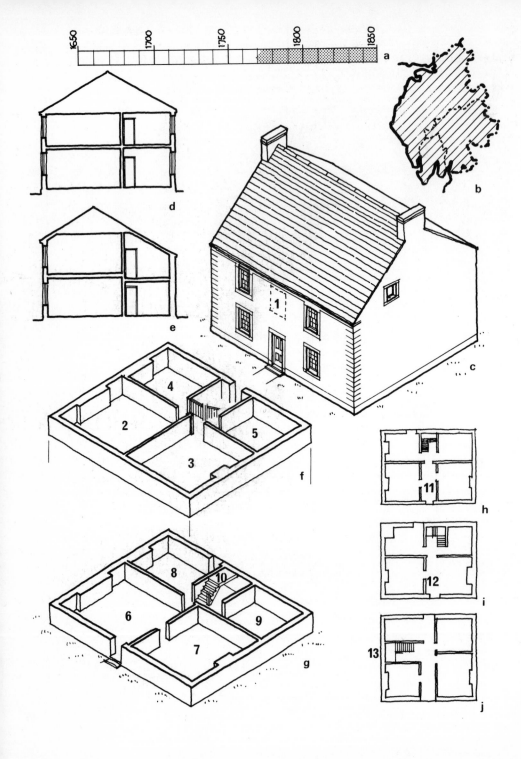

a

1650 1700 1750 1800 1850

b

c

d

e

f

2 4 3 5 1

g

6 8 10 7 9

h

11

i

12

j

13

side the front door. Another modification was to add a bay at one end to act as a servants' wing or to provide extra service and storage space without detracting from the neat symmetry of the basic plan. For the double-pile plan retained the central doorway and symmetrically disposed windows of its predecessor, and in the larger houses, especially those with a lobby, the central doorway actually was in the centre, though in the smaller examples the door was still offset to increase the size of the parlour. In the larger houses there might be three bedrooms on the front giving three windows on the first floor, but in the smaller houses the same elevational effect was achieved through the use of a blind window.

Examples of the double-pile plan may be found in all building materials over the whole of the Lake Counties. They include examples at Small House level dated from about 1770 and such houses were built right through the 19C, adopting and discarding strict Palladian, Greek Revival and Gothic Revival details on the same basic room arrangement.

28. Double-pile plan
a. time scale showing period of use from about 1770 to 1850
b. map showing widespread distribution
c. sketch showing door near the centre of the main elevation, roof covering a plan two rooms in depth, position for blind window (1)
d. cross-section showing eaves at same height front and back; roof is normally carried on purlins supported by the gable walls and one intermediate wall
e. alternative cross-section showing transition from continuous outshut plan with lower room heights and lower eaves at the rear
f. first-floor plan with four bedrooms (2, 3, 4, 5) and the load bearing intermediate wall so close to the middle of the plan as to discourage use of a centre window and to suggest use of blind window
g. ground-floor plan with front door opening straight into living room (6) off which is parlour (7); behind are the back kitchen (8), dairy (9) and staircase (10)
h. alternative plan showing use of lobby lit by a fanlight over the front door to improve the comfort of the living room (11)
i. plan showing how a door off-centre allowed a larger parlour (12)
j. alternative plan showing staircase on a gable wall (13)

Cottages

The cottages of the Lake Counties had a very short life within the vernacular zone. Buildings intended for the occupation of cottagers, i.e., families with little or no stake in the land – labourers, quarrymen, charcoal burners, tinkers – or for widows or paupers appeared in permanent materials towards the end of the 18C and passed over the polite threshold scarcely a century later.

It seems likely that until well into the 18C the economy and social organisation of the Lake Counties was not such as to produce a numerous class of cottagers; farms were generally small, most farmers were yeomen or had as secure a customary tenure as Border conditions would permit, the farming operations required little outside labour, social customs could accommodate family misfortunes. The region was poor in comparison with many other parts of the country, but the poverty was evenly spread, there was less material difference between most of the local landowning families and their customary tenants than between, say, an East Anglian magnate and his scores of hired hands. There are few cottages mentioned as such in the 1603 survey of the Barony of Gilsland. However, during the 18C, conditions changed: enclosures and changed methods of farming depleted the ranks of the 'statesmen', forcing many off the land; mines and quarries created a demand for labour in remote districts far from established settlements; textile manufacture began to move from the farmhouse to the weaver's cottage and then to the water-powered factory with its industrial settlement; new industries like iron smelting created still further demands for labour and increased the demands on old-established cottager activities like coppicing, charcoal burning, and bobbin making. These changing conditions meant a need for simple cheap accommodation in villages and towns to serve agricultural and industrial requirements at a time of swiftly expanding population anyway.

When constructed in materials permanent enough to survive cottage designs fell into three groups: single-storey cottages recalling earlier Small House plans, compressed or miniature versions of existing Small House plans, and the single-fronted cottage version of the double-pile plan.

29. Single-storey cottage – Riddings, Nichol Forest, Cumberland

The single-storey cottage is essentially a two-room dwelling, like the Scottish 'but and ben'; and the earlier examples can hardly be distinguished from the smaller two-unit Small Houses. Typical examples have a living kitchen containing the principal or only fireplace and a parlour-bedroom with, in the later examples, a subsidiary fireplace. There might be a third room serving as a scullery or as a workshop. These rooms were open to the roof or to a ceiling which might also provide loft space over one of the rooms. A door somewhere near the middle of the front wall and a window to each room completed the minimal architectural organisation. Examples are not particularly numerous and are found most frequently near the Scottish Border (reflecting no doubt the influence of a common Scottish house type) and near the mines of north eastern Cumberland, reflecting a pattern common in many mining districts. Where the cottager was in fact a small-holder keeping one or two animals, perhaps on land acquired from the waste, then the cottage formed one end of a short range of buildings, at first glance like a long house but actually without cross-passage or intercommunication.

Cottages single storey

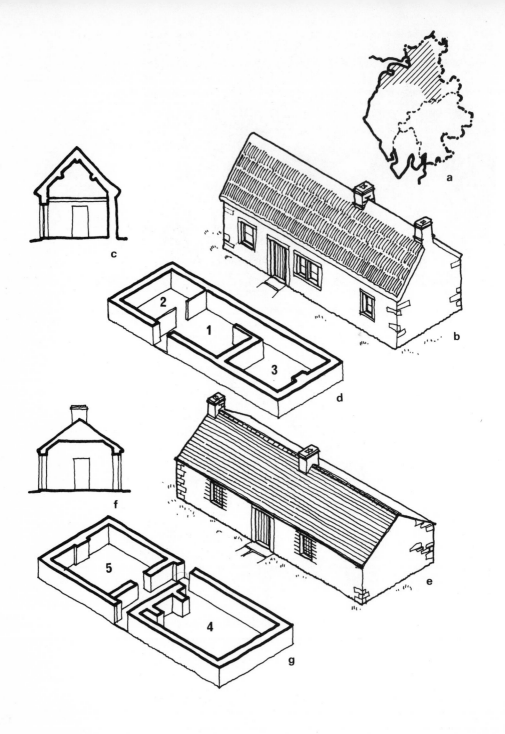

31. Cottage as a miniature Small House –
Glasson, Cumberland

Cottages miniature

A more common group of cottage designs found throughout the
Lake Counties is the two-storey cottage which appears to be a
scaled down version of its Small House neighbour. Included in
this group are the gable entry cottages with one room and perhaps a tiny pantry on the ground floor and a bedroom within the
roof space above. The inglenook with its enclosing partition and
its fire window resembles at a rather smaller scale the arrangement at the hearth of a 17C Small House. The pantry and narrow
staircase or companionway-ladder concealed in a cupboard is a
token of the inner room of a Small House. The bedroom at the
upper level might contain the firehood and would be lit by a
small window under the low eaves at floor level or by a window
in the opposite gable. Also in this group are the rather later
cottages which have two rooms on the ground floor with a staircase between and leading to two bedrooms set partly in the roof
space. Such a cottage would have a principal fireplace in the
living-kitchen and a subsidiary fireplace in the diminutive par-

30. Single-storey cottages
a. map showing concentration near the Border
b. sketch (based on an example at Newtown C) showing an elongated
three-unit building
c. cross-section with loft space over bedroom reached by ladder
d. plan with living room (1), bedroom (2), kitchen or parlour (3)
e. sketch showing a two-unit arrangement (based on an example near
Bewcastle, C)
f. cross-section showing the rooms open to a ceiling at collar level
g. plan with living room (4) and bedroom (5)

a

c

b

3

2

1

d

e

f

g

h

lour. The front elevation, consisting of a doorway set off-centre and windows on each side, is at first glance similar to that of a common Small House type, a very compact version of the two-unit house, but these cottages are even smaller in dimensions and appreciably later in date, reflecting the decline of a plan type and the rise in cottager standards of accommodation. Another plan type within this group is that of the 'one up and one down' cottage found singly, in pairs, or in short rows. These have a single living room downstairs and a bedroom above a single fireplace, and a ladder-like staircase connecting the two floors. This was evidently considered the normal standard of cottage accommodation in the second half of the 18C for it

32. Cottages as miniature Small Houses
a. map showing widespread distribution
b. sketch showing a miniature two-unit house with door off-centre and rooms on each side
c. section showing house one room deep but two full storeys high
d. ground-floor plan with living room (1) and parlour (2), staircase between rising to two bedrooms. Often a small pantry is added to or incorporated in the rear (3)
e. sketch showing an early 'one up and one down' cottage
f. plan with the single living room entered directly from the front door and the single bedroom reached by a steep ladder-like stair in a cupboard in a corner of the room
g. sketch showing an even simpler type of cottage with a single room on the ground floor and a loft above lit by a gable window in the wall opposite the chimney stack
h. plan showing the single living room entered from the gable and a steep wooden spiral staircase rising to the loft above

34. Terrace of single-fronted cottages at Haverthwaite, Lancashire

provided the basis of the squares and crescents proposed by Adam for Sir James Lowther's model village in 1756, and many cottages of this plan were included in the modified scheme which was constructed at Lowther (W) after 1767.

Cottages double-pile single-fronted

The double-pile farmhouse has been shown as the culmination in vernacular Small House design through its compactness, its economy, its spaciousness within small compass. The same qualities may fairly be ascribed to its diminutive, the single-fronted two-storey cottage.

A dwelling of such a plan has a living kitchen occupying the whole narrow frontage; behind there is a small scullery or pantry together with a staircase which rises steeply in two

35. Cottages double-pile, single-fronted
a. time scale showing period of use from about 1790 through to 1850 and beyond
b. map showing widespread distribution with concentration in mining areas of West Cumberland and industrial Furness
c. sketch showing a reflected pair of cottages with doors together and a blind window above (1)
d. cross-section showing two full storeys' height
e. first-floor plan of a reflected pair with the main bedroom (2), small bedroom (3), party wall at blind window (4)
f. ground-floor plan with living room (5), pantry (6) and staircase (7)
g. alternative ground-floor plan showing a reflected pair with doors apart
h. alternative ground-floor plan with living room (8), scullery (9) as part of a terrace
i. first-floor plan with two bedrooms

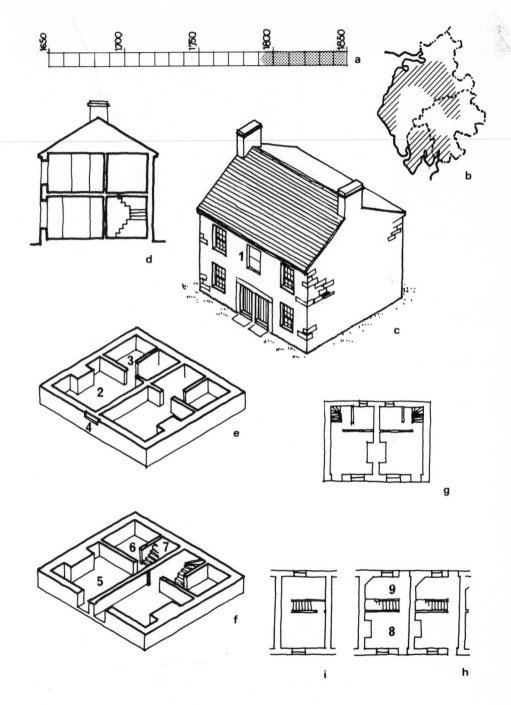

flights and many winders to the upper floor, which has two bedrooms corresponding to the two rooms below. The larger room
on each floor has a fireplace; entrance is by a front door directly
into the living kitchen; such a cottage, in fact, resembles a
double-pile house cut in half.

Cottages of such a plan may be seen attached to a conventional
double-pile farmhouse so as to provide accommodation for a
farm labourer and his family. They may be found, in the villages,
built as reflected pairs, i.e., with the two front doors together
(when there may be a blind window and decorative plaque above
the pair of doors) or with the fireplaces combined in a single
stack and the front doors apart. They may be found in the mining districts of West Cumberland in terraced rows.

Developments of this cottage plan led to an even greater
depth and taller rooms without any increase in frontage.
Standards of accommodation improved under the double stimuli
of increased prosperity, with rising living standards, and increased governmental interference in house design, with greater
uniformity. Anonymous terraces designed according to nationally understood patterns and governed by nationally inspired
legislation; uniform materials brought cheaply from distant
sources on railways or in steamships; both combined so as
virtually to eliminate the vernacular qualities in even the
humblest dwellings.

In a predominantly agricultural region like the Lake Counties, farm buildings must rank with domestic buildings in any study of vernacular architecture. Indeed, the study of farm buildings is, if anything, more urgent than the study of farm houses, the greater number of such buildings being especially vulnerable as they are abandoned or converted to other uses under the pressure of modern farming methods. Ironically, the long agricultural depression (1880 to 1940) left many of the older buildings intact though neglected, and the most serious phase of demolition and conversion has only recently begun; large numbers survive just as they are coming to be appreciated.

Farm buildings fit into a vernacular zone generally similar to that established for Small Houses. The very few medieval survivals such as the tithe barn in Carlisle (probably 15C) were built for people or institutions of high status. The rather larger number of 16C and early 17C farm buildings such as those of Yanwath Hall (W), Park House Farm, Heversham (W), or Kirkby Hall (L), are associated with the Large Houses of people of some local importance. The rebuilding of yeomen's houses from the late 17C on was followed shortly afterwards by some reconstruction of farm buildings. However, the great wave of investment in such buildings occurred in the hundred years or so from the later years of the 18C to about 1880 or 1890. The phases in agricultural development have already been mentioned: the establishment of a system of communal farming in open fields, the crystallisation in the age of the 'statesmen', then replacement by a more scientifically based farming of enclosed fields. They were reflected in the design of farm buildings, at first too insubstantial to survive, then developing as specialised buildings and finally culminating in designs of some ingenuity and not inconsiderable cost.

The principal farm buildings found in the Lake Counties, as in most parts of England and Wales, are the barn, the cow-house, the stable, and the granary; subsidiary buildings included various loose-boxes or 'hulls'; specialised buildings or combinations of local significance were the bank barn, the field barn and the horse engine house, or 'gin-case'. All were combined with farmhouse and farmyard in one of several recognisable arrangements to comprise the buildings of the farmstead.

The *barn* was designed for the storage and conversion of grain crops. The sheaves of corn (chiefly oats and barley in this region) were carted into storage bays during the harvest and then, throughout the winter, they were gradually threshed by hand flail on the wood or stone-flagged threshing floor, the straw being used for bedding, for thatching, or even as fodder, the grain being taken, after winnowing, to be ground at the mill or fed to horses or cattle. Threshing by this process required a tall open space above the threshing floor, a set of tall, outward opening barn doors for light and access, and a porch or canopy for protection against the rain. Winnowing required a through draught from doors preferably of unequal size. Storage was best provided in a tall space with limited ventilation through narrow slits or small holes. As the productivity of the land improved and machinery was used first for winnowing and then for threshing, the bulk of the crop was stored outside in the 'stack garth', storage bays in the barn being reduced to lofts over stable and cow-house, though the threshing floor was retained for occasional use. Originally hay was kept in lofts over cow-house or stable, in a haybarn with open sides and no threshing floor, or in a Dutch Barn, simply a roof on posts. But later, as a proportionately smaller grain crop was steam-threshed in the stack garth, the corn barns were used to store hay. Now, with the popularity of silage pits, even this use has diminished.

The *cow-house* or 'byre' was designed for the accommodation of oxen and milking cattle during the winter months or at milking time. The arrangement of separate feeding and manure passages, common in other parts of the country, is seldom found in this region. Instead, the cattle were tethered in pairs, separated by a low partition, the 'scale board' of timber or stone, backing on to a manure passage and drain, and fed from behind into individual feeding boxes and a manger rack. There was seldom any window, light and ventilation coming from the upper half of the split door; the beams of the loft floor were very low, and with the limited ventilation the hay above kept the cow-houses hot and dusty throughout the long winter months.

The *stable* became increasingly important during the 18C as

---

36. Aerial view of Kirkbampton, Cumberland, showing farmstead layouts (Aerofilms Ltd.) (a polygonal horse engine house may be seen in the centre foreground)

oxen gave way to horses as the source of motive power on the farm. A stable had separate stalls for each horse, stout wooden partitions being reinforced against kicking at the rear and raised high against biting at the head. There was also usually a loose box in the stable. Above, the loft contained hay or straw, but the stable always had at least one window, was taller than the cow-byre, cleaner and better ventilated. An upland sheep

---

37. Farmstead layouts

A. Longhouse arrangement
  a. sketch of single elongated range, main chimney stack near the middle of the building, entrance to cross-passage running behind the chimney breast, farm buildings at 'lower' end
  b. typical plan with house (1), cross-passage (2), cow-house (3), barn (4)

B. Laithe-house arrangement
  a. sketch showing main chimney stack at one end of range, no cross-passage, farm buildings usually at 'upper' end of house
  b. typical plan with house (1), barn (2), stable and loft over (3), cow-house (4)

C. Parallel arrangement
  a. sketch showing two parallel ranges of buildings, one including the farmhouse
  b. typical plan with house (1), stable with loft or granary over (2), barn (3) with loft over cow-house (4)

D. L-shaped arrangement
  a. sketch showing buildings arranged about an angle; house is shown attached but may equally be separate
  b. typical plan with house (1) attached to stable (2), cow-house (3), cartshed and granary over (4), barn (5)

E. U-shaped arrangement
  a. sketch showing buildings and house in a U-shape; alternatively the house may be quite separate
  b. plan with house (1), cow-house (2), stable (3), barn (4), loose box (5)

F. Courtyard arrangement
  a. sketch showing enclosed farmyard, in this case incorporating the back of the farmhouse
  b. plan with house (1), carthorse stable (2), cow-house (3), barn (4), carriage horse stable (5), traphouse (6), cartshed with granary over (7), pig-sties, shelter shed, etc. (8)

G. Farmyard with bank barn
  a. sketch showing all major farm buildings incorporated in the bank barn
  b. typical plan with house (1), loose boxes (2), cow-house (3), cartshed (4), stable (5), and barn over

H. Scattered arrangement
  a. sketch showing haphazard layout
  b. plan with house (1), cow-house and stable (2, 3), barn (4), pig-sties (5)

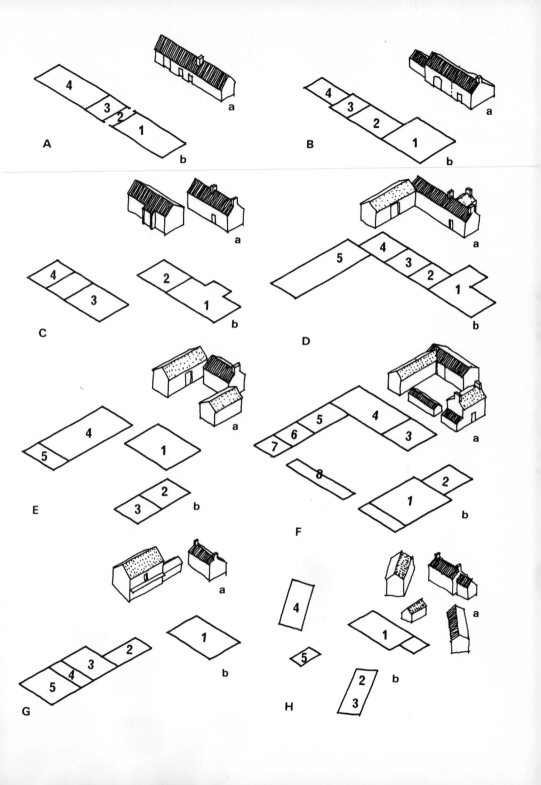

A

B

C

D

E

F

G

H

a

b

farm would have a separate stable for the pony or 'nag' on which the farmer rode when 'shepherding'. A rich lowland farm would have one stable for the Galloways and Clydesdales which pulled the plough and another for the riding horse and the pony which pulled the trap.

The *granary* is often mistaken for a bedroom as, in the Lake Counties, it was always on the first floor and reached by an external stone staircase, had domestic type windows, and sometimes had a fireplace. The granary accommodated grain or flour (and later other feeding stuffs such as imported Indian Corn) in wooden chests or 'kists' or in piles on the close-boarded floor. Quite often the granary was placed over an open-fronted cartshed, ventilation of the granary floor helping to reduce mildew. Sometimes it was placed over a stable. Usually, on a small farm it was attached to the house, and many a visitor to the Lake Counties in former days may recall the sound of rats scampering from the granary over the bedroom ceiling.

In the relatively severe climate of the greater part of the Lake Counties cattle could not winter satisfactorily in the fields or even outside in the farmyard, and so many farmsteads included various loose boxes or 'hulls' in which young cattle could be housed during the winter months, treading manure several feet deep so that, at spring time, they almost touched the ceiling beams. In the Lake District there were also 'hogg houses' in which the weaker or more valuable sheep could be wintered. The minor buildings of the farmstead include pig-sties (now rarely used to house pigs), occasionally a kiln in which corn gathered green from a short damp harvest season could be dried, or a malting kiln for conversion of barley.

Eight types of *farmstead layout* may be distinguished, six of them related to the size of farm, one unrelated, and one probably found in England only in the Lake Counties.

The simplest layout, and possibly the oldest, is that which consists of a farmhouse and range of buildings attached together in a long line, cow-house, barn and stable extending from the lower or service end of the farmhouse and linked to it by way of a cross-passage. It is obviously related to the '*long-house*' tradition and in some few examples actual or recent intercommunication between house and cow-house has been confirmed, but generally the two portions of the range of buildings show different periods of building and have separate access for cattle and humans. Sometimes the house appears later than the farm buildings and even with a late 18C date may still retain the cross-passage; sometimes the farm buildings are later than the house, a tall, substantial range of barn and byre dominating oddly a small, low-ridged house. Sometimes a service room intervenes between house and buildings. But in all cases the spirit of the longhouse arrangement has been followed. Usually there is some differentiation in colour or quality of material between domestic and agricultural portions, the house being whitewashed and the building left as rubble, or even the buildings whitewashed rubble and the house a squared, knapped or ashlared face in natural stone; this may mean that an entrance doorway at one end of a cross-passage, having dressed jambs and a decorated lintel but with a loft or granary above, is 'claimed' by whitewash away from the cow-house and towards the house itself.

The extent of the farm buildings associated with the medieval longhouse is at present unknown, and further information depends on excavation of known sites, but where a boulder plinth continues from the house along the base of a rebuilt wall the implication is that they were short, certainly no longer than the house, and in size appropriate to the few cattle, the small amount of grain, and the single horse which was all the poverty of land in the Lake Counties could justify.

Small farms of the 18C were often organised in the *laithe-house* plan. This arrangement is seen in its purest form in the Central Pennines, around Halifax, and especially during the late 18C and early 19C; the farm buildings are attached to the upper end of the farmhouse, without a cross-passage and often without intercommunication, but the whole farmstead consists of one line of buildings. In the Lake Counties, such a farmstead, serving perhaps 30 acres, would consist of a farmhouse, a barn with threshing floor, and a loft over a stable for two horses, and a cow-house with tying for ten or a dozen cattle. Generally buildings of this form were erected at one time, the house being two storeys in height and a common roof running over the whole range. Although superficially resembling the longhouse the pattern is fundamentally different and the arrangement is unlikely to be earlier than the 18C.

On the larger and later farms the farmhouse was set apart from the farm buildings to reflect a social distinction which became increasingly important but which never gained complete control in this region.

In the *parallel* arrangement, the farmhouse and a range of farm buildings were set in a parallel row, the farm buildings consisting of barn, cow-house, stable, and the farmhouse probably incorporating a cart-shed and granary. The association of the granary with the house and the upper floor of the house is long-standing, as it dates from the period in which grain, fleeces, and other valuable items of farm produce were kept in the house, and in the private, upper end at that. The more utilitarian or offensive parts of the farmstead were separated, though the outlook from house to midden which was still maintained showed that a pleasing prospect was not yet a major planning factor.

The larger farms of 50–150 acres or so, with correspondingly larger farm buildings, used *L-shaped* or *U-shaped* layouts, with the farmhouse either completely detached or linked to granary or stable. The farm buildings included a substantial barn (or more than one barn where acreage and productivity had increased significantly over the small 'statesman' farm), a stable for three or four horses, and a separate stable for riding horses, one or two cow-houses, tying perhaps two dozen cattle, two or three loose boxes for young cattle, a cartshed and granary, and a pigsty. The farmhouse of the continuous outshut or the double-pile plan would be linked to the farmyard but with a front door and principal rooms facing away from the noise, dirt, and smell of the yard.

On the largest farms of all, over 250 acres of cultivated land or meadow, the farm buildings would be so extensive as to range around a *courtyard*. This might result from a process of accretion where more barns, cow-houses, etc., were built as more land was enclosed and taken into cultivation, or it might result from deliberate planning where an estate adopted a model plan for the farmsteads established as a deliberate policy on newly enclosed land. The farmhouse on such a farmstead would almost always be detached, approached by its own access road; it would turn its back on the farm buildings, but, in the planned farmsteads, would be axially related to the buildings. The whole might even be related in some way to the landowner's country house; the Gothick fantasies near Greystoke with their turrets and pinnacles were evidently intended to be incidents in the design of the landscape viewed from the windows of Greystoke Castle. At this rate farmbuildings and farmstead layout are no longer part of vernacular architecture.

Bank barns

A bank barn is a farm building which combines a conventional threshing barn at an upper level with a cow-house, stable, etc., at a lower level. The true bank barn was always sited *along* the contours of a natural or artificial slope; the variant bank barn was sited *across* the contours. From a field or track at the upper

38. **a.** and **b.** views of opposite sides of a bank barn near Cartmel, Lancashire

39. 'Spinning gallery' on barn near Coniston, Lancashire

level a short ramp allowed access for carts into the barn; the lower level opened into the farmyard where the horses and cattle could be exercised and watered and into which their dung could be led. The upper level included a threshing floor; the barn doors were usually protected by a canopy and sometimes had projecting wings on each side of the ramp; the small, domestic-sized winnowing door opened precariously from the threshing floor high up the wall at the opposite side; there were trapdoors through which straw could be dropped to the animals below. At the lower level there was often a cartshed immediately under the threshing floor, a cow-house at one side, and a stable with taller ceiling at the other. In many examples the doors into these spaces were protected by a continuous cantilevered canopy; no doubt this did allow the farmer to pass from door to door under cover but that would hardly be a matter of much importance to a hardy farmer accustomed to tramping miles across the fells in any weather; its main purpose was probably to protect stable and cow-house when the upper part of a split door was open for ventilation.

Bank barns are very numerous in the Lake Counties. At least 400 are known and there might well be two or three times that number still surviving. The bank barn is the predominant type of farm building in most parts of the Lake Counties and especially in the west and south west. On the flat part of the Solway Plain it was little used, but even here some brick bank barns were erected on artificial slopes. In the extreme south there are instances in which a slope was carefully flattened for a conven-

---

40. Bank Barns

a. time scale showing period of use from about 1730
b. map showing scarcity of examples in the north of the region; cross-hatched portion indicates use of canopy in south
c. sketch showing the barn placed *along* the slope, access to lower level from the farmyard
d. sketch of opposite side showing access to upper level by ramp from road or field
e. cross-section with lower level built into slope, ramp to upper level, canopy over barn entrance (1), pentise canopy sometimes provided at lower level (2)
f. plan at upper level with threshing floor (1), storage bays each side (2, 3), outward opening barn doors (4), winnowing door (5)
g. typical plan at lower level with cow-house (6), cattle tethered in pairs in stalls (7), cartshed (8), stable (9), with horses tethered individually in stalls
h. sketch showing development of outshuts alongside ramp
i. sketch of bank barn variant placed *across* the contours with access to cow-house or loose-box at one end of the building

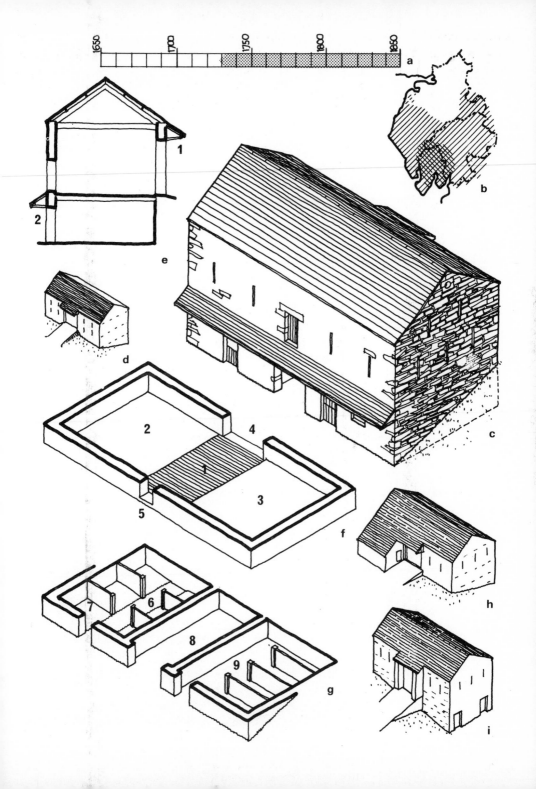

a

b

1

2

e

d

c

2 4

1

5 3

f

7 6

8

9 g

h

i

tional barn instead of using the bank barn form. In the Eden
Valley there was mixed use; sometimes bank barns and flat
barns were used on the same farmstead. Continuous canopies
were common in the south west but rare elsewhere. The earliest
reliably dated bank barn is part of a house and barn combination
at Nettleslack in Martindale, Westmorland, bearing a plaque
dated 1735, but a barn dated 1681 at Barwise Hall, Hoff, Westmorland, may have been of this form. The latest dated example
is of 1904 near Duddon Bridge in Lancashire, but buildings of
this type may have been erected up to 1914. There are many
dated examples between these two extremes.

In England the true bank barn is almost peculiar to the Lake
Counties. One or two examples have been noted in the North
Yorkshire Moors and in Devonshire and examples are known in
Scotland but the building type is densely packed into a quite
precisely determined part of the north-west of England; it is not
found in other parts of England or in Wales where topography
and farming methods are very similar to those of the Lake
Counties. The variant bank barn, with restricted accommodation for cattle or horses entered through the gable at the lower
end of the building, is more widely spread and was especially
common in the south-eastern part of the Lake Counties.

One other type of combination farm building which made use
of sloping ground was the barn intended primarily for storage of
hay, with ramp access to the upper level but with storage bays
dropping down to the lower level as 'sink mows' flanking a cow-
house which had doorways or hatches allowing the hay to be
drawn in and fed to the cattle. In principle such barns are related

41. Field barn or 'field
house', near Sebergham,
Cumberland

42. Horse engine house, Newbiggin, Cumberland

to the 'self-feeding barns' popular in the United States during the 19C.

The field barn or 'field house' also made use of sloping ground. **Field barns**
A field barn was an outlying building with accommodation at a lower level for young cattle kept loose or, occasionally, for tethered milking cattle, and a hay loft at an upper level often dropping as a sink mow to the lower level. Hay could be swept from the upland meadows into the field barn with the minimum of labour; it was fed during the winter to the cattle or to sheep who were penned alongside. Manure was then led from the field house down to the cultivated fields. Where an ancient farmstead was located in the village it was obviously economical to decentralise such buildings rather than lead all the crops into the farmstead and then carry all the manure back up to the fields. Most field barns appear to be of late 18C or 19C date and were presumably erected when the fells were enclosed and allotments of land made to the old farms. Field barns are especially plentiful on the Pennine slopes but may also be seen in the Lake District.

One more farm building type which is found in the Lake Coun- **Horse engine houses**
ties, though by no means exclusively so, is the horse engine house, called locally the 'gin case'. The early stationary thresh-ing machines were sometimes turned by wind, water, or steam power, but most were operated by the horse engine, a device

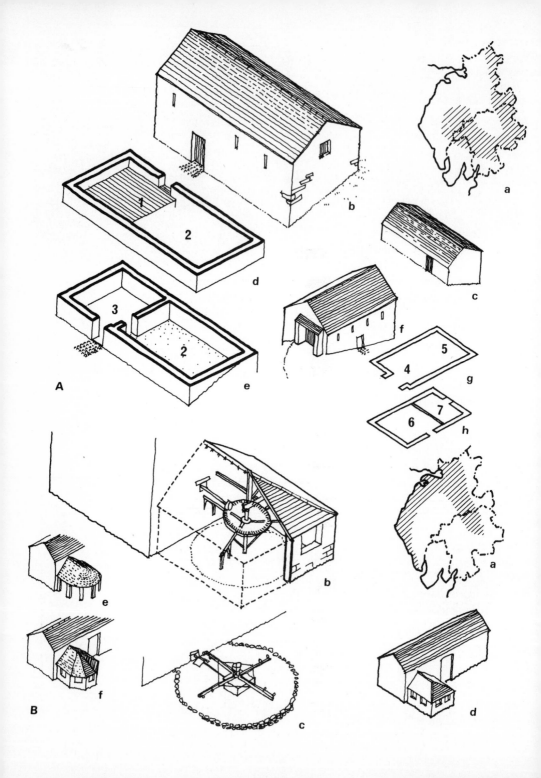

A

1
2
3
b
d
e

a
c
f
g
h
4
5
6
7

B

b
c
d
e
f
a

whereby horses walking a circular track turned a crown wheel, pinion, and so the shaft of a threshing machine. In one version, probably the earlier, the horses walked underneath the gearing and machinery and horses were enclosed in a building which projected from the barn and had a square, polygonal or apsidal termination. The building was well ventilated by windows or by gaps between piers supporting the roof. After portable steam threshing machines had superseded the stationary machine the horse engine was used to power the multiplicity of cutting, crushing, and mixing machines needed in high farming. The later horse engines were made of iron, had a less cumbersome mechanism which the horses could step over and required no building cover. These leave no architectural evidence of their use apart from the small hole through which the shaft penetrated the barn wall, but there are about 40 or 50 of the older type of horse engine house still to be seen on the larger farms in the Eden Valley and on the West Cumberland coast lands.

43. Field barns and horse engine houses
A. Field barns
  a. map showing principal use along Pennines and lesser use in Lake District
  b. sketch showing field barn placed *along* the contours, access at lower level to loose-box
  c. sketch from opposite direction, access at upper level to hay loft
  d. plan at upper level with loft (1) and 'sink-mow' dropping to lower level (2)
  e. plan at lower level with lower part of sink-mow (2) and loose-box (3)
  f. sketch showing a field barn placed *across* the contours, access at lower level to cow-house
  g. plan at upper level showing loft (4) and sink-mow (5)
  h. plan at lower level with cow-house (6) and lower part of sink-mow (7)
B. Horse engine houses
  a. map locating area of use in Eden Valley and coastal plain
  b. sketch showing horse engine with overhead gearing
  c. sketch showing sweep type gearing without horse engine house
  d., e., f. alternative forms of horse engine house

Urban
Vernacular

In the Lake Counties, as elsewhere, there is a difference between urban and rural vernacular architecture. In the towns, plans were modified where houses served also as shops and where they were units of continuously built-up frontage on long narrow plots. Buildings were made tall to provide adequate space on a congested site or to give an impressive appearance for a shopkeeper or professional man. In this region, especially, the construction of urban houses was unusual in retaining conventional timber framing of a type which has disappeared entirely from the countryside, and, indeed, may never have existed there.

Appleby, Kendal, and Carlisle are three towns of special interest: Appleby as a planned new town of the early 12C whose framework has been slowly extended over the years, Kendal as a town of long narrow medieval plots developed as 'yards' of closely packed stone houses behind a timber frame facade, and Carlisle as the former walled city overwhelmed by industrial expansion in the 19C. There are several others which would repay a visit: Hawkshead for tightly packed clusters of houses, some timber framed; Ulverston and Broughton-in-Furness for evidence of 18C industrial prosperity at a time when vernacular traditions were still strong; Cockermouth, Wigton and Whitehaven for the spaciousness of commercial success during the same period; Penrith for its several market places and its dignified town houses overlooking the churchyard. Certain villages also have some urban qualities, e.g., Church Brough (W) as the shell of a medieval military town, Burton in Kendal (W) with its projecting storeys, reminders of a timber-frame tradition, Dalston (C) and Brampton (C) with continuously built-up frontages dating from prosperity as minor textile centres. The holiday towns – Keswick, Windermere, Ambleside – are less interesting to the student of vernacular architecture except for the long survival of local building materials when they were romantically fashionable as well as conveniently available.

The very attractive town of *Appleby* consists of two parts: the older foundation on the east bank of the River Eden straddling

44. Appleby, Westmorland, view along Boroughgate with 18C houses on medieval plots

the road between Westmorland and Yorkshire by the Stainmore pass and the new town on the opposite bank mounting the hillside between the Church of St Lawrence and Appleby Castle. The names of the two principal streets recall the two foundations: Bongate where the villeins retained their original rights and obligations and Boroughgate where the burgesses of the new town enjoyed their privileges as citizens. Boroughgate was the market place, and a market is still held in its lower portion; the town records testify to the constant battle to prevent encroachment on the market place and to ensure reasonable cleanliness and adequate drainage. Long, narrow plots lead at right angles from this market place down to the river or back to the parallel street of Doomgate and the linking 'wiends'. There is no trace of the medieval property to be seen, though one building in Boroughgate, now a chemist's shop, has mullioned windows, continuous label moulds, dormer windows to a steep-pitched roof, and has been recorded as having upper crucks inside, and another building on The Sands, now a private garage, has a cruck truss inside, a steep pitched roof, formerly thatched, and signs of mullioned windows in the wall. There are one or two 17C buildings on Boroughgate with surviving or blocked mullioned windows, but the main impression is of 18C and early 19C houses, tall, imposing, well proportioned and neatly detailed, the White House with its 'Gothick' doorway and window heads being the most sophisticated though still recognisably of the district. At the head of Boroughgate, on the Wiends and on Doomgate the early 19C cottage development

91

45. Kendal, Westmorland, Highgate with typical very unobtrusive arched entrance to a 'yard' on the left hand side of the street

took place, two-storey narrow-frontage cottages retaining the character of the town with their red sandstone walls, slated roofs, and continuous frontages. Expansion during the later 19C led Appleby towards its railway stations – as at Penrith and Kirkby Stephen – and the steep parallel streets rising above Bongate have semi-detached villas and terraced cottages of the period when vernacular qualities had been all but lost.

The older part of *Kendal* consists of the long north-south street of Kirkland/Highgate/Stricklandgate raised above the River Kent with Finkle Street and Market Place diverging to join Stramongate and so the Stramongate Bridge across the river. The town is overlooked by the motte of Castle Howe on the west and the shell keep of Kendal Castle on the east. Buildings of all periods from the late medieval to the present day are compressed along the street frontage and along the 150 or so 'yards', narrow passages giving access to buildings stretching along the original plots and at right angles to the street – down to the river or up to the fellside, both features of some importance during Kendal's long period of eminence as a textile centre. While often assumed to be defensive in origin, this pattern can, of course, be seen in many old towns and is more a method of 18C property development than 14C protection.

In Kendal as indeed in any town one should look above the modern shopfronts to the older houses and shops from which they have been converted. Many of the buildings are three-storeyed; most appear to be built of exposed or rendered limestone (recent use of slatestone is a misguided sop to an assumed tradition) and a number appear to be timber framed. Their construction is revealed by jettied upper storeys as in the Fleece Inn, Highgate, and the Globe Inn, Market Place, or by the thin walls with window frames close to the surface and little inner reveal to be seen through upper floor windows, as at Titus Wilson's shop or Farrer's Tea and Coffee Shop in Highgate. The timber is concealed behind rendering and roughcast, probably contemporary with the 19C window replacements, but one method of timber cladding, possibly unique, may be seen in the cast iron panels, one dated 1853, on Branthwaite Row.

Important individual houses include the medieval hall house, Castle Dairy, now hemmed in by other property on Wildman Street, though once isolated. The real flavour of Kendal, however, comes in the 18C and 19C cottages in the yards with their rough limestone walls and Lake District Slate roofs, a flavour which has been recaptured in their recent more sanitary replacements at the south-eastern end of Highgate.

Carlisle was established as a military town, its castle and walled settlement forming a bastion to guard the western gateway between England and Scotland. Medieval Carlisle appears to have had a fairly open development, large parts of the walled city being in gardens and orchards or in walled enclosures of which the chief was the Cathedral and its related monastic buildings. Houses and shops were spread along the streets which led between the three gates and the triangular market place. Very little survives to give any impression of the property in medieval Carlisle but the timber-framed Guildhall suggests that the city, like Chester, Shrewsbury, and Kendal, was once full of tall, narrow, jettied, timber-frame houses and shops.

The last siege and military occupation of Carlisle was as recent as 1745, during the second Jacobite Rebellion, and so the existence of castle and walls continued to influence development long after it had ceased to do so in other such towns. Within the walls the open spaces were filled, but only gradually as the important local landowners retained the gardens of their town houses. However, Georgian houses may be seen in, say, Abbey Street and above the modern shopfronts of Fisher Street; they are mainly of brick but some are of sandstone and with Lake District Slate roofs. At the same time ribbon development was beginning on the less congested sites outside the city gates.

To meet the influx of labour attracted to industrial Carlisle in the 19C there was first subdivision of old property and new construction in yards and gardens until congestion of the old

46. Carlisle, Cumberland, Spencer St., terraced houses of 19C

town reached its maximum in 1841. During the second half of the 19C land became available on the outskirts, especially after the new bridge made Denton Holme accessible; at first it was developed in small parcels, typically a courtyard of 'back to back' dwellings, some facing the street, others facing the yard, which was reached through a tunnel; the long, narrow shapes of the old fields dominated the layout. After about 1865 and under the influence of an increasingly powerful Board of Health the courtyard development was abandoned and the unit of development became the terrace of narrow frontage 'two up and two down' or 'tunnel back' houses. These were of brick with slated roofs. The workers' suburbs on the west and south of the medieval city, which had now lost its walls, followed this pattern, an arbitrary collection of streets followed old field patterns with odd changes of alignment. On the east of the city most of the land was held by three estates, those of the Duke of Devonshire, the Earl of Lonsdale and the City Corporation and they were able to exercise the landowner's power of planning control to create an attractive sequence of crescents, terraces, avenues and squares.

After about 1880, the larger scale of development, the closer control imposed through the Public Health Acts, and the increasing use of railway-borne materials such as Welsh slate eliminated practically all trace of vernacular quality in the houses of the City.

Apart from the domestic and agricultural buildings which form the greater part of the wealth of vernacular architecture in the Lake Counties there are several types of small industrial buildings, some of them quite early in date, whose interest and significance has been revealed through the work of the industrial archaeologists. Chief among these are the mills, mainly water mills, developed and perfected to grind corn but adapted in design to provide power for textile trades. Also interesting are the kilns devised to dry corn, to malt barley, to convert wood into potash, or to burn limestone into lime. Of great historical interest, though perhaps less interesting architecturally, are the buildings erected for early metal working – furnaces and forges – and the buildings related to mining and quarrying which served these industries. In some instances the process or the machinery dominates the design of the building but generally it appears that the early craftsmen had to draw upon whatever traditional designs and skills seemed appropriate to provide the buildings for new industrial enterprises until a body of specialist design had developed. In early industrial vernacular, as in domestic and agricultural, a vernacular zone may be detected between the period from which no permanent buildings survive and that in which specialised buildings were designed by professional architects or engineers.

Probably the oldest type of industrial building in the region is the *corn mill*. Although most surviving mills appear to date from the late 18C and the 19C many probably occupy earlier sites. There were some windmills (sites of about 40 are known) of which the stump of a tower remains but no complete windmill survives, and the known sites lie mainly on the exposed coastal plain, especially between Whitehaven and Carlisle. The great agricultural reformer J. C. Curwen incorporated a windmill to drive farm machinery at Schoose, his model farmstead near Workington, but the whole operation was beyond the vernacular level. The steep hillsides and consistent supplies of water made water-powered mills more reliable than windmills, and indeed water remained competitive with steam throughout the 19C and

47. Akebank Mill, near Loweswater, Cumberland

some water-powered mills may well be in use even today.

The simple water mill as perfected in the early 19C was usually arranged on three levels: the lowest level contained the horizontal drive from the water wheel and the gearing which converted it into a vertical drive to the intermediate level, where the sets of mill stones were located, while the topmost level, often partly in the roof space and between upper crucks, was used as storage space for the raw material. The water wheel might be external (though protected by a roof) or internal, but required a narrow, easily controlled headrace, a bypass, and a tailrace. It became usual, especially during the 19C, to incorporate a drying kiln or a malting kiln at one end of the mill; fired by charcoal the kiln did not need a chimney. Near the mill there may usually be seen the miller's house, a conventional Small House of the period with a stable and cart shed and with a small range of farm buildings where the miller, like so many of his neighbours, was a part-time farmer. A mill was as a rule a simple rectangular building of the size and proportions of a barn, but even if the wheel and water courses have disappeared, a mill may easily be recognised by its position on a slope, its two

---

48. Water-powered corn mills

a. sketch showing alignment across the slope and with headrace (1) and tailrace (2) fo water wheel; example based on Viver Mill, Hincaster (W) after D. R. Moorhouse

b. plan at topmost level with hoppers for grain (3) and chute to kiln (4)

c. plan at intermediate level with main milling floor (5), tiled kiln floor (6) and loft over cartshed (7)

d. plan at lower level with water wheel (8), gearing (9) and fire hole for kiln (10)

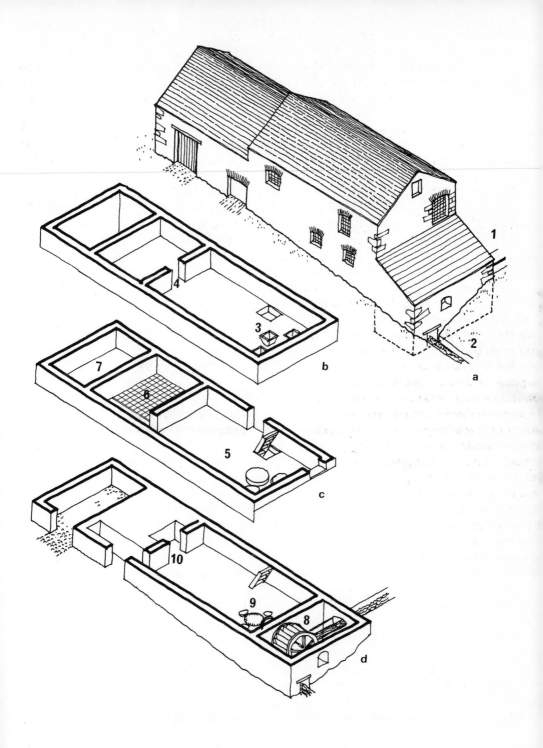

1

2

4

3

b

a

7

6

5

c

10

9

8

d

and a half or three storeys of small domestic-sized windows, and by the absence of chimneys.

The further development in the 18C of the ancient textile industries in many parts of the Lake Counties but especially near Kendal led eventually to the design of factory buildings. As in many parts of the country the earlier textile industry was simply a widespread domestic activity organised by clothiers who routed the raw material through the different processes from farm to farm and cottage to cottage, collecting the product for sale elsewhere. This industry had produced the famous Kendal Green and the socks on which Wellington's soldiers had tramped up and down Spain in the Peninsular Wars. The improvements begun in the 18C were to change the industry from a domestic to a factory-based activity.

Early examples of buildings for textile manufacture such as that which survives in Kirkby Stephen were simply houses in which handpowered spinning jennies or mules were collected in one building. An early building type was the fulling mill or 'walk mill' in which heavy wooden hammers were driven by water power to beat and consolidate the cloth before it was hung on tenterhooks to dry in the open air. A few examples survive, but the name can be seen on maps especially in the southern Lake District. *Factories* in the modern sense began as small rectangular buildings, three or four storeys in height, with machinery driven by water wheels by way of belting and shafting, and in appearance like large corn mills except for the extra storey and the much larger proportion of windows. The buildings were usually deep, especially where spinning mules were to be accommodated; the tall, closely spaced domestic-shaped windows were supplemented by sloping rooflights to help illuminate the top floor. These small mills were bound to the source of their water power on what now seem remote and improbable sites. They were eventually superseded by the great steam-powered factories like the former Shadden Mills at Carlisle, built as early as 1836, and a magnificent work of architecture though still retaining some little vernacular quality in its materials and detailing. However, several of the small early mills remain active in the Lake District dales.

The old-established textile industry, and the skilfully conserved coppice timber of the southern Lake District encouraged the water-powered bobbin-making industry. The wooden bobbins were turned on lathes in a square, usually single storey, building with many windows (it has been suggested by Marshall and Davies-Shiel that one can estimate the number of lathes by counting the number of windows). Nearby there was a *coppice timber barn* or drying shed, a slated roof raised on round, or, later, square stone piers rather like a hay barn. Several such establishments remain, one or two still in operation, in the southern dales.

Coppice timber was grown mainly for conversion into charcoal. The curious bee-hive-shaped charcoal burner's huts illus-

49. Part of linen mill, Cockermouth, Cumberland

trated by H. S. Cowper were used by some of the earlier writers on vernacular architecture to demonstrate the primitive forms of domestic construction through these possible late survivals. The huts were similar in shape to the stacks in which wood was converted into charcoal; they were also generally similar to the contemporary bark-peeler's huts. All were the response to the nomadic life of these craftsmen, buildings being required while a copse was being worked, then abandoned as the operation moved elsewhere.

As charcoal and iron ore were available together, conditions were right for the development of the iron and steel industry, especially in Furness. The early hand-powered bloomery hearths in use until the mid 17C have left no architectural trace. Bloom smithies in which a set of bellows was driven by a water-wheel were more efficient and required buildings of a sort to accommodate the smelting furnace and the water-powered tilt hammer, but, again, little remains to be seen above ground. After 1711 *blast furnaces* were introduced. These required a complex of buildings depending on the tall stone furnace fed with ore from the top by way of a ramp and having one aperture at the base for the huge water-powered bellows and another deeply vaulted opening through which the two tons or so of molten iron and the slag could be tapped; nearby were the charcoal storage sheds, huge barns in which the large quantities of bulky charcoal needed for the process could be kept dry; round about there were various other stores, offices, stables, etc. The brittle cast iron

---

50. Some industrial buildings
A. Blast furnace layout, based on Duddon Bridge ironworks (after Davies-Shiel)
  a. charcoal store, filled through high-level openings at the rear
  b. offices
  c. loading platform, may have shelter shed over
  d. blast furnace
  e. area for tapping metal and running into pigs
  f. position of water-powered bellows
  g. diagrammatic section through furnace, with firebrick lining (1), 'tuyeres' for draught (2) and space for access and tapping (3)
B. and C. Various forms of kiln (after Davies-Shiel) all built into a bank
  a. early potash kiln, a deep 'pot' with tiny entrance near base
  b. later potash kiln with iron pot lining
  a. early lime kiln with wide mouth at the top
  b. later lime kiln tapering towards the top
D. Sheds for storing coppice timber, e.g., at bobbin works
  a. earlier type with rounded piers
  b. later type with square piers
E. Three-storey textile mill, machinery belt-driven from water wheel

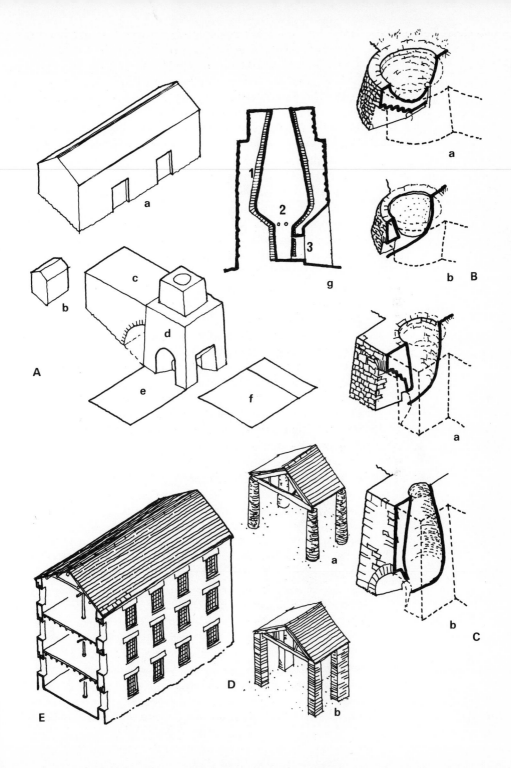

had to be converted into malleable wrought iron in a finery forge like that recently excavated at Stony Hazel, Rusland, nr. Coniston and consisting of a tall hearth with water-powered bellows and trip hammer and charcoal and iron stores. Eventually these early industrial sites, secluded among the wooded valleys which ensured power and fuel, were superseded by the much less attractively located steelworks of Workington, Millom Barrow, etc., scientifically designed and gaunt and dramatic rather than pleasant to look upon. However, the remains of the 18C and early 19C building groups remind one that in these new industrial processes without direct precedent the designers had to call upon the traditional, the vernacular, building construction which was really all that was available to them.

Charcoal was also essential for producing potash which in its turn was a constituent of the soap used for domestic purposes and as part of the fulling process in finishing new cloth. Birch twigs or bracken were roasted over a charcoal fire in an iron pot set in a hollow stone-walled depression to produce the potash. A few *potash kilns* have recently been discovered; they may be recognised by their shape of a squat slightly tapered stone cylinder set into a bank and with a small firehole at the base.

The early *lime kilns* were rather like these potash kilns except that there was a deeper stone-lined pit dropping to the small aperture reached from the outside by a tall but quickly contracting access chamber. Limestone and coal were tipped from the top and then burnt in alternate layers until the quicklime could be raked out at the bottom. From the mid 19C onwards a more efficient inverted kiln used, lined with firebrick and tapering from a wide, rounded base upwards to a narrow neck at the top. Lime was of course extensively used on the sour acidic land of the fells and such limekilns are plentiful in the limestone-bearing parts of the Lake Counties, located usually where an outcrop of the rock forms a bank or cliff face.

There was a considerable range of industry active in the Lake Counties during the 18C and early 19C at this vernacular level. All the processes required buildings of some sort and while many of these buildings have fallen into ruin many more surely remain to be discovered, both overgrown and hidden in remote dales and also exposed but unrecognised in the towns and villages. In many of these buildings the design was certainly subordinate to the process or machinery contained but in others qualities ranging from the robust to the elegant may be detected, suggesting that when better understood they may be appreciated almost as much as their domestic or agricultural counterparts.

The Christmas Card picture of a Lakeland farmstead shows whitewashed stone walls, tall cylindrical chimneys and slated roofs. This impression, hardly correct for the majority of surviving buildings in the area of the National Park, let alone of the Lake Counties as a whole, could reveal nothing of the intricacies of crucks or various forms of roof construction, nor would it acknowledge the strength of a tradition of timber-frame construction surviving in the towns and possibly not represented in the countryside. Above all such an apparently timeless picture is in fact a relatively recent one. Until 300 years or so ago the vernacular buildings of the Lake Counties may have been rough huts of turf and rubble walls with turfed or heather-thatched roofs from which the few slated and stone-walled churches, towers, and bastle houses stood out prominently in the villages and the wattle and daubed timber-framed town houses suggested a difference between urban and rural cultures.

Cruck construction is the most primitive form of assembly of which there are significant remains in domestic agricultural and industrial vernacular buildings. Huge curved wooden blades (locally called 'siles') were inclined together, joined at the apex, held lower down by a collar or tie beam, and raised on padstones. They carried a ridge purlin, side purlins, and, by an extension of the tie beam, the wall plates, so that the roof loads were taken directly through the feet of the cruck blades to the padstone and so to the ground. In the purest (and most primitive) form of cruck construction the walls served only to keep out the weather and carried no loads other than their own weight.

Cruck-framed trusses

It is generally assumed that early cruck-framed buildings were enclosed in some sort of timber-framed wall or by large wattled panels and, although no complete example from this phase has been discovered in the Lake Counties, a partially timber-framed and weather-boarded wall has been recorded in a cruck-

Cruck-framed trusses

51. Cruck trusses at Gt.
Orton, Cumberland

framed barn at Hawkshead Hill Farm. Most walls around crucked
buildings, however, were built of stone and it must have been
gradually understood that such walls, when properly constructed, could carry the wall plates and thus parts of the roof load.
Other walls were of clay and the useful structural properties of a
stout clay wall were similarly employed in due course. While
a building of full cruck construction had cruck trusses at each
gable and at each of the intermediate bays the increasing use of
the structural properties of the enclosing wall meant that the
end crucks could be eliminated and the intermediate crucks

raised higher and higher up the walls until they became similar in function to conventional roof trusses, the short curved feet being tenoned into a tie beam as an upper cruck. The cruck tradition died hard and late in the Lake Counties; many barns, especially in the clay walling districts had full cruck trusses made of the most flimsy and unsuitable timber long after other forms of construction must have been known. Several mills of late 18C or early 19C date have been found with well-formed upper crucks giving an uninterrupted wall and clear floor space on the top floor.

The blades of cruck trusses could be made from whole tree trunks approximately matched or could be accurately matched by halving a large tree trunk in a saw pit; in either case great skill would be needed in selecting a tree with the right amount of curve. Timber of adequate quality, plentiful in some English counties, must have been scarce in this region; there are few of the gracefully matched blades of Herefordshire or Worcestershire, none of the richly decorated members of cruck trusses found in some remote Welsh counties, and many very irregular and spindly examples. Some crucks on the Solway Plain were crudely jointed out of two pieces in order to make some sort of a curve.

Many cruck trusses show evidence of a change of pitch from the 45° or more used in thatched roofs to the 30° or 35° of slated or stone-flagged roofs. Subsidiary members and blocking pieces were used to carry the purlins, and long thin cruck spurs, tapering and dovetail housed into the blades, were employed as ties rather than as brackets like the much heavier cruck spurs of, say, Monmouthshire houses.

Several different details were employed at the ridge, in each case the heavy ridge purlins being cradled in some sort of support. The problem of securing this member was evidently exaggerated by the local carpenters, especially when other forms of roof construction dispensed with the ridge altogether. There was also some variation in the link between cruck blades and side purlins by way of wind or sway braces. These light straight or curved members, when provided, served either to counteract horizontal movement or racking or they helped to reduce the unsupported length of purlins. But in many instances they were not provided at all and the cruck trusses seemed satisfactory without them.

Cruck trusses were not erected piece by piece but were framed up on the ground, reared into an upright position, then manoeuvred on to a permanent base until ridge, side purlins,

105

and wall plates could be put into place. Near the base of the
cruck blade one may sometimes see the elongated slot for the
pike or crowbar which helped to give leverage for the first lift
and then was pushed through to act as a lifting bar while the
foot of the blade was placed on its padstone. In the collar may be
seen the hole for the ropes which helped to pull up the truss to its
final position and acted as a guy to stop it falling right over.

There is little or no evidence whereby the simple undecorated
cruck trusses of the Lake Counties can be dated. A few upper
crucks have been found in houses bearing dates or dateable
evidence of the late 17C or early 18C according to their size,
status, and general character. Many members especially in the
cruder work have been re-used. The technique may have sur-
vived in humble construction to the end of the 18C or even the
early 19C on the evidence of the flimsy truss in cottages demolished near Silloth (C) or the substantial upper crucks on
mills of South Westmorland and North Lancashire.

Roof trusses

Roof trusses carried on load-bearing walls in the region appear
to derive either directly from cruck construction or from a tradition of using a king post to carry a heavy ridge purlin. There are
no precisely dated examples, but roof trusses do survive in Large
Houses or buildings on the border of the vernacular zone from

52. Cruck construction
a. diagram to show how roof loads are carried by cruck frame to the
   ground
b. two-bay cruck-framed building with closed crucks (1), open cruck
   (2), cruck blade (3), tie beam (4), collar (5), ridge purlin (6), side
   purlin (7), wall plate (8)
c. diagram to show sequence of rearing crucks
d. full cruck with side purlins carried on blocks, blades rising from
   ground level
e. full cruck with side purlins carried on outer blades (9)
f. raised cruck with blades supported on the wall
g. upper cruck with blades rising from the lower tie beam
h. upper cruck with collar
i. yoke at ridge
j. blades halves and crossed at ridge
k. ridge purlin carried on king block on saddle
l. collar yoke
m. blades halves or tenoned at ridge
n. gable end of a ridge purlin carried on a short king post supported on
   a spreader and steadied by curved braces
o. and p. side purlins trenched into blades with straight or curved
   braces (after Moorhouse)
q. cruck tie locating wall plate which is supported by wall

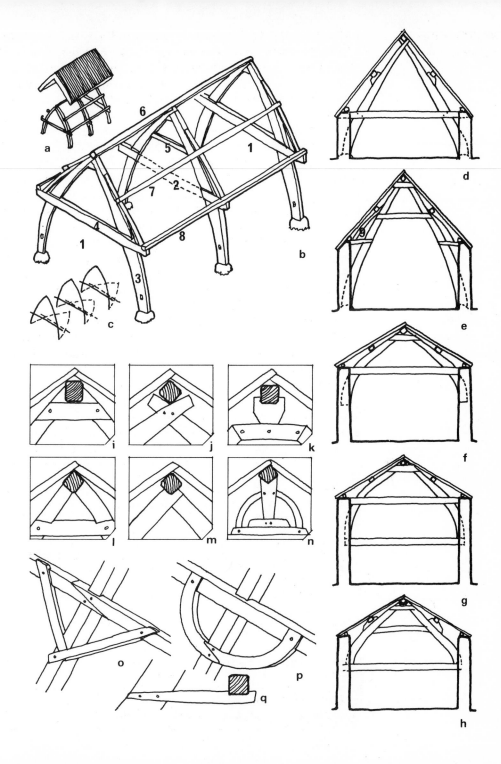

the medieval period. At Preston Patrick Hall (W) there are two
quite remarkable sets of roof trusses, one set having a king post
rising from a cambered tie beam and steadied by curved struts
with the purlins carried on short thick stubs, the other having
an unbraced king post and purlins clenched between duplicate
rafters. Arch-braced collar beam trusses include examples at
Kirkby Thore Hall (W) and the fine range over the hall at Yanwath (W) where a short king post rises from the collar and a 15C
date is probable. At the Stonehouse, Naworth Park (C) believed
to date from the early 16C, a heavy tie beam with its upper side
cambered supports a king post and angle struts and gives some
evidence of a ceiling. In 17C houses of wide span, such as
Mansion House, Eamontbridge (W) or the central block of
Hutton-in-the-Forest (C) a tall king post acts almost as a tree
trunk to sprout layers of inclined struts bracing the principal
rafters. At all stages there persists the use of angle braces running longitudinally between tie beam and ridge purlin.

During the 18C there was a tendency for roof trusses to pass
out of use for domestic buildings, purlins being carried by the
gable and intermediate walls, but they remained necessary for
barns and other undivided agricultural or industrial buildings.
Usually some variation of the basic triangle of tie beam and principle rafters was used, having a light collar (used probably
as a locating member in framing and raising the truss) or with
angle struts. Sometimes re-used cruck blades were employed as
principal rafters, the blades being inverted and re-jointed but
showing the dovetail halvings for collar or tie beam as well as the

53. Roof trusses
a. cutaway isometric to show purlins carried by gable wall and by
   intermediate trusses supported on side walls
b. cutaway isometric showing purlins carried on gable walls and an
   intermediate wall and continued along an outshut
c. truss, probably 14C, based on Preston Patrick Hall (W)
d. arch-braced collar-beam truss, 15C, based on Yanwath Hall (W)
e. king post roof truss, probably 16C, based on Naworth Stonehouse
   (C)
f. truss, 17C, with king post and struts, based on Hutton-in-the-
   Forest (C) and Mansion House, Eamontbridge (W)
g. struts supporting the ridge purlin longitudinally as found in many
   roof trusses 14C–16C
h. tie beam and light collar roof 18/19C
i. as **h.** but made of re-used cruck blades
j. tie beam truss with angle struts 18/19C
k. simple tie-beam truss 18/19C
l. 19C truss with wrought-iron bar as king post in tension
m. 19C king post truss with strapped joints

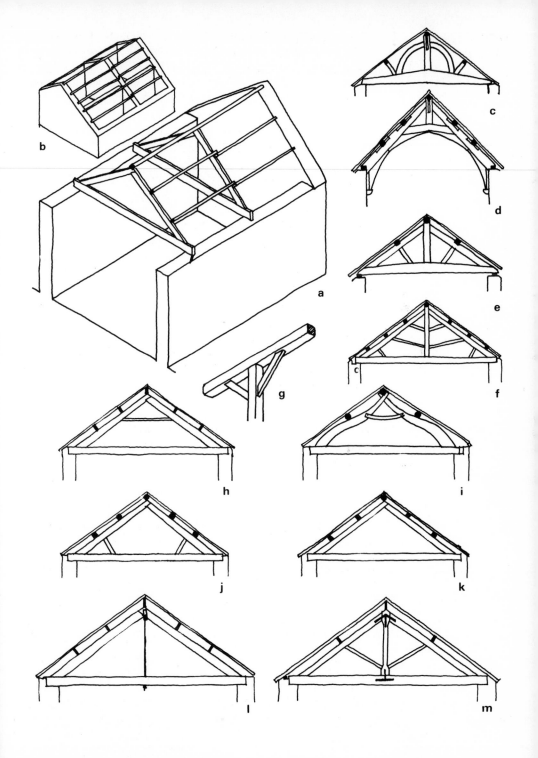

a

b

c

d

e

c

f

g

h

i

j

k

l

m

curved shape indicating the previous use. In all cases a heavy ridge was used and side purlins were supported on the backs of the principal rafters, not tenoned in or passing through. During the late 19C the king post returned to favour for the larger spans but this time as part of a scientifically designed truss with the king post recognised as a tension member, bolted or strapped to the tie beam, rather than as a compression member resting on top of it.

Walling materials

Both clay walls and brickwork were used in some parts of the Lake Counties at various periods, but stone walls, whether of sandstone, limestone, slatestone or cobble, predominate and, exposed or rendered, help to maintain the rugged character of much of the landscape.

In the Eden Valley and along the Cumberland coast Permian and Triassic *sandstone* provided a sound and easily worked walling material, either pink and rather hard, or red and so soft that finish and carved detail eroded away. The red sandstone buildings in and around Penrith were considered so unusual that Celia Fiennes thought the town made of brick. Construction of the sandstone walls appears to have been quite conventional; walls were usually between 1 ft. 9 ins. and 2 ft. thick, consisting of an outer and inner face of worked or selected stone with a packing of smaller pieces and waste, bonding being obtained by means of 'through' stones at intervals of 3 ft. or 4 ft. vertically and 2 ft. or so horizontally; quoins and door and window dressings were built up by a mason in worked stones, the remainder being raised by the waller. Until lime mortar became generally available late in the 18C stones were bedded in clay though they might be pointed in lime mortar, and it is the leaching of clay exposed in a broken wall which hastens its ruin. Walls on the older and smaller houses were raised on a boulder plinth, a row of huge rounded stones, morainic deposits cleared

---

54. Stone wall construction
    a. sandstone wall with a projecting 'through' (1); limestone walls similar though with a less regular material, often rendered
    b. slatestone wall with 'watershot' tilting towards outer face (2), 'dry' surface without mortar (3), packing of interior with small flakings laid dry (4)
    c. cobble wall with split cobbles giving a fair face (5), sandstone or slatestone bonding and through stones (6)
    d. clay wall showing mixture of pebbly clay and chopped straw with straw lacing courses (7). These walls were rendered and whitewashed

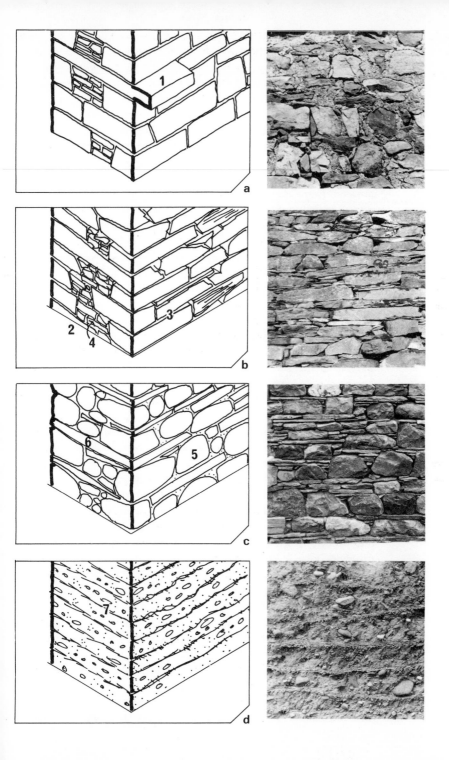

from the fields and possibly surviving from earlier buildings.

Running in a belt around the sandstone and also inland from Morecambe Bay there are deposits of *carboniferous limestone*. This ranges in character from compact angular blocks to rough striated stones heavily encrusted with fossils. Neither type is particularly easy to use in walling and cannot readily be worked if at all; sometimes quoins and lintels roughly worked with a hammer may be seen, but more often such dressings as were provided were made from sandstone imported from adjacent districts. One detail found especially with carboniferous limestone in barns and other outbuildings but also found in the gable and rear walls of houses built of this material is the use of projecting 'through' stones; these, sometimes in a superior quality of stone, project at intervals like a series of broken ledges.

Within the heart of the Lake District the hard olive green or grey-purple *slatestone* is characteristic. This includes fieldstone or stone quarried on the spot as used for older and humbler buildings, and the knapped stones and quarry waste used for dressings and generally for the later buildings. Walls built of this material were commonly laid 'watershot', i.e., with a distinct tilt towards the outer face, a technique which certainly helped to direct any water driven into the wall back out of harms way but which also helped to give a fair face to the wall, the stones splitting naturally at an obtuse angle between bed and face. Slatestone walls often appear to have been laid 'dry', i.e., without mortar or any other bedding, relying on skilful selection of interlocking pieces of stone for stability and plastered inner surfaces to keep out draughts in houses; there developed a technique in the later 19C of providing a mortar strip set back from the outer face of the wall to preserve an illusion of dry walling. However, it is hard to decide to what extent dry walling is an ancient technique in building houses and other structures in the Lake Counties, notwithstanding its universal use for field walls, and to what extent the older examples result from loss of a clay or earthen bedding material. Walls, mainly of the late 19C, and including the Silurian rock of the Windermere district, made of carefully split and knapped stones and sawn quoins and other dressings, represent the walling technique at its best, though the rough fieldstone walls marching over the fells may represent the technique at its most attractive.

Walls built partly or wholly of *cobblestones* are common throughout the Lake Counties. The cobbles are rounded water-worn stones midway in size between the pebbles of the seashore and the boulders cleared from the fields; they were available nearly everywhere, either from the river beds or from the soil, the debris of the last, quite recent, Ice Age. They were used widely on the Solway Plain and on the West Cumberland coast wherever better quality stone was scarce, and they were used quite widely in the Lake District, providing body to a wall in which slatestone throughs provided stability. Cobbles could be split so as to give a fair face to the wall but they could not be worked in any other way; a thick bedding of clay or some sort of mortar was required in which the rounded cobbles could be set; the walls were usually thick and distinctly battered; they required dressings of slatestone, sandstone, or use of limestone at quoins or openings. Their colours, ranging from a gleaming white to a dead black, could add further variety to the wall texture though cobble walls with wide vulnerable joints were often rendered and whitewashed for improved appearance and better weather resistance.

Hundreds of *clay-walled* buildings remain in Cumberland and as many more probably incorporate clay in later rebuildings. They survive in the section of the Solway Plain between Silloth and Carlisle but they were once common over a much wider area. Although none of the clay-walled buildings examined appears to be more than 300 years old and most are much more recent, the technique, and the related technique of turf walling, may once have been widespread in the Lake Counties. The material was a mixture of clay, small stones, and chopped straw and was laid in courses three or four inches thick between thin layers of straw. There are accounts of the construction of clay-walled houses in the early 19C showing this to have been a communal activity involving digging, mixing and kneading the clay, forming rolls which were unrolled course by course along the walls, the whole operation being rapidly completed. Although this was quite different from the slow, more careful process of building the cob walls of SW England, clay walls raised on boulder footings and protected by a plaster rendering have proved to be sound and permanent. The technique was obviously related to cruck construction; the quickly built walls probably originated as non-load-bearing screens around the cruck trusses, but substantial two-storey double-pile houses with outer and partition walls raised to carry purlins have also been recorded in this form of construction.

As one might expect, the predominant roofing material found throughout the region is Lake District Slate, but sandstone flags, purple Welsh slate and thatch have also been used.

Roofing materials

113

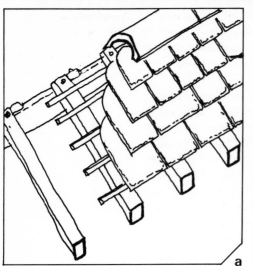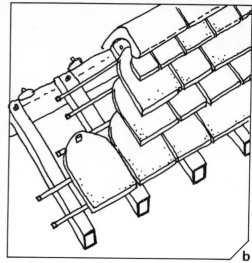

55. Roof coverings

a. Lake District slate laid in diminishing courses and random widths; each slate is rounded at the head, squared at the foot, and fixed with one nail or peg

b. Sandstone flag roof covering, also laid in diminishing courses and narrow widths and with rounded heads; fixing by wooden peg or sheep's bone over the laths rather than through them

Lake District Slate, extensively quarried from the 18C to the 20C, was, of course, used locally beforehand and is still occasionally won for roofing purposes. It was formerly known as blue slate and was exported by way of coastal shipping to provide durable and fire resistant roofing on the more important buildings in London and other cities accessible to shipping in the 18C. The colour ranges from grey through blue to green but the lichens attracted to the material enhance a grey-green effect. Locally there was a wide range of quality in use, from thin carefully split slates in superior buildings to the rough irregular more natural-looking slates used on humbler buildings in the vicinity of the quarries. Individual slates were chipped to give a rounded upper end (like stone flags but unlike most Welsh slates) and were pegged to rough laths; they were laid in diminishing courses, the larger and wider slates at the eaves and the shorter and narrower slates at the ridge. Usually there was a shaped sandstone ridge to cover the topmost courses but where such stone was especially difficult to obtain heavy slates were cut to give interlocking ears as 'wrestler slates'.

114

Sandstone flags were quite extensively used in the middle and upper Eden Valley, where the local stone splits easily to form thick and heavy and fairly durable slabs or 'flagstones'. In the Pennine communities of the Alston district millstone grit flags of similar characteristics were used. The flags were laid and coursed in a similar manner to Lake District slates but usually to a lower pitch and giving a deeper texture and more massive scale to the roof. Sandstone flags may often be seen as the lower few courses of a roof otherwise covered in a different material, usually Welsh slate; this may be a relic of an earlier practice of using such flags as a damp-proof course over a stone or clay wall and under thatch.

Scarcely any *thatched* roofs remain visible but there are several instances of thatch concealed beneath corrugated steel or asbestos sheeting, and, on the evidence of topographical writers and draughtsmen of the late 18C and early 19C, thatch was widely used, especially on the Solway Plain, in NE Cumberland, and, to a lesser extent, in the Eden Valley. Straw thatch was probably used but the few surviving examples include heather or ling. None which has been examined is in a sufficient state of repair to give much information on thatching techniques.

The *Welsh Slate* roofs display thin uniform blue or purple slates laid to regular courses. As the local slate was plentiful it is unlikely that Welsh Slate became competitive until after the railway network was established between about 1840 and 1880. When used on older buildings, therefore, Welsh Slates may be regarded as a replacement for an inferior material such as thatch. Indeed the districts in which Welsh Slate was most extensively used correspond with those in which thatch survives or was known to have been used. Plain tiles and pantiles were virtually unknown in the Lake Counties until after 1918 and, again, where used on old buildings, appear to be a substitute for an original thatch roof.

**Roofing and
chimney details**

As slates and flags were the predominant roofing materials used in the Lake Counties it is hardly surprising that nearly all roofs were gabled and few had dormers or valleys, since neither material lends itself to these variations from the simplicity of a basic roof shape. The few hipped roofs responded to the fashion of the early 19C in which the roof had to be minimized in the design of the building. Gables were usually finished with a plain close verge but barge-boarded projections are found in 19C roofs, raised copings or parapets in the better quality buildings of the 18C, and crow-stepped or 'corbie-stepped' gables in the

Roofing and chimney
details

56. Roofing and chimney
details – house near
Troutbeck, Westmor-
land, has a cylindrical
chimney stack corbelled
from a corbie-stepped
gable wall and with
slate water tabling.

57. Roofing and chimney details
a. raking gable coping with gutter at eaves draining into a rainwater head
b. plain close verge, the normal in the district
c. barge boards with deep projection at verge, 19C
d. crow-stepped or 'corbie-stepped' gable used especially with slate-stone walls in Lake District, detail shown
e. projecting ground-floor chimney breast; an oven projection is rare
f. chimney breast corbelled out from first floor
g. chimney stack corbelled out near ridge as when taking a hooded chimney inside
h. normal gable stack with an internal stack placed *forward* of the ridge, as often happens with a hooded chimney backing on to a cross-passage wall
i. medieval chimney stack based on an example at Yanwath Hall (W)
j. two-flue stack in squared masonry as found in superior houses
k. cylindrical stack, usually made of small limestone pieces, found especially in Furness and South Westmorland
l. water tabling of projecting slates or stone slabs
m. as l. but slabs set into a raking groove
n. lead flashings used at the junction in 19C and later
o. section through a stone ridge
p. 'wrestler slates' used in place of a ridge
q., r. rain water heads in lead or cast iron
s. raking gable coping with plain finish
t. raking gable coping finished by a kneeler
u., v. upper and lower views of a typical kneeler

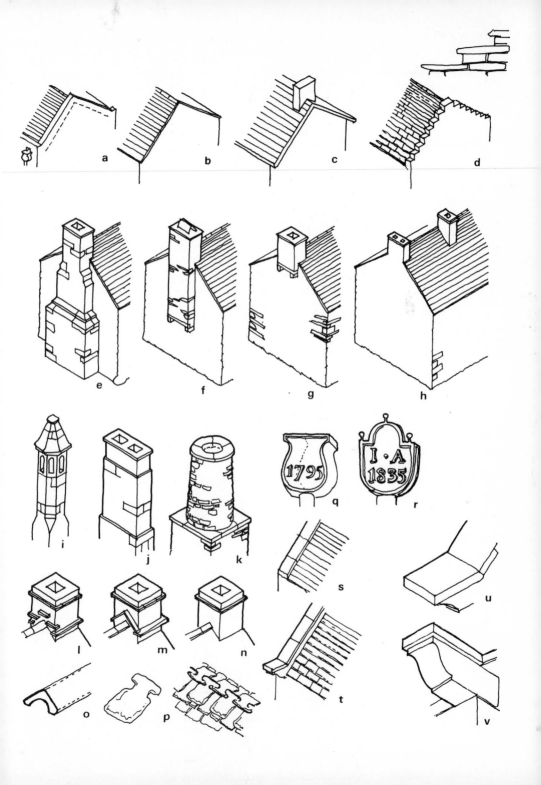

Lake District and the Scottish Border. Gable copings or parapets were usually finished by a projecting and moulded kneeler,
giving a fixing as well as an architectural termination. This
detail is found in many stone walling districts, especially in the
Pennines, and gives the opportunity for some inventiveness as
well as a misuse of classical precedent by the vernacular masons.

Chimneys vary considerably in prominence: the Small House
of the 17C and 18C with its single hooded flue required only one
chimney stack rising through the roof or at the gable and set
forward to avoid the ridge purlin; earlier and larger houses
sometimes had a substantial chimney breast and chimney stack
projecting from a gable wall; another detail found especially in
the southern Lake District involved a partially projecting gable
chimney stack rising from the first floor and carried on shallow
corbels. The joint between chimney stack and roofing material
was always vulnerable and, before lead became cheap enough
and plentiful enough for such use, this joint was protected by
projecting stones or slates in water tabling. The tapered cylinder
chimney stack rising from a square base is often associated with
the Lake Counties, and fine examples may be seen at such houses
as Town End, Troutbeck (W) but its use is in fact confined to a
relatively small part of the region where the carboniferous
limestone presumably could not be used to make satisfactory
rectangular stacks.

The heat of the fire and the force of the weather attack a
chimney stack in a way to which stone is especially vulnerable;
many houses therefore, including the humblest and least well-
constructed examples, have modern brick stacks replacing some
earlier material.

It would be quite wrong to dismiss the designers of our vernacular buildings as mere functionalists, intent only to enclose simple domestic, agricultural or industrial processes in the cheapest building envelope available. When the occasion required they built substantially, they built to last, and they built with an eye or an instinct for satisfactory proportions. They also built with a pride which led to the use of architectural details, external and internal ornaments, the display of initials and dates, and, generally, to the completion of their building designs through the use of the fashionable architectural embellishments of a rather distant Society. For this reason alone, the design of windows, doorways, cupboards, panelling, etc., should be briefly examined – and in so doing useful indicators in dating these simple buildings will hopefully emerge.

Decoration was, of course, helped or hindered according to the walling material at hand. In those districts, especially of the Eden Valley, where sandstone was available, moulded jambs, classical architraves, carved or incised ornaments, etc., of good quality could be provided and with relative ease. The hard pink gritty sandstone was satisfactory to work and resistant to weathering, though the more plentiful soft russet Penrith and St. Bees sandstone was very easy to work but quickly lost its edge or laminated away. In the carboniferous limestone district around Kendal some quality in worked stone was also possible, though elsewhere in this belt, and especially around Kirkby Stephen, the fossil-laden limestone was quite impossible to work. In the slatestone area of the heart of the Lake District the material was rough and inhospitable except that in the second half of the 19C the use of quarry waste with better tools and machinery meant that some very precise carved work could be achieved. On the Solway Plain, clay was suitable only for the crudest walling and the plaster coating was never developed as a base for painted or pargetted decoration; there was, however, a good deal of transport of sandstone dressings into adjacent districts and also use of such dressings with brickwork.

58. A range of architectural details, house at Sebergham, Cumberland

Windows and window frames

Variations in window design included shape, division, mouldings and glazing. Changes in window shape from tall to long then square to tall again can readily be observed and reflect the influence of fashion and convenience on room heights. The tall first-floor room or solar of the medieval Large House suggested the tall window with pointed or traceried arch which may be seen, e.g., at Asby Rectory (W). The ground floor open hall of such a house suggested a squarish window of two or three lights compressed between a high cill and the low eaves of a steeply pitched roof. When an intermediate floor was inserted or houses built with two storeys throughout (after about 1550), the rooms were almost inevitably low and so windows were made horizontal with several lights. The early Small Houses with low eaves or with a lofted principal room have such windows. In the late 17C and early 18C, Large Houses, such as Mansion House, Eamontbridge (W) or Moresby Hall (C) were given tall windows under Renaissance influence to light tall rooms in compact multi-storey houses; but contemporary Small Houses still had low ceilings and the square window became popular, perhaps as a compromise, and usually set alongside the single-light 'fire window' which lit the inglenook. However, rooms, ceilings and windows began to rise in height again as Renaissance influence penetrated to Small House and even Cottage level, until, early in the 19C, it was succeeded by the Gothic Revival and a return to the original sequence. The division of windows varied with shape and size. Small upright slit windows as used at ground-floor level in medieval buildings were undivided but the bigger windows to the more important rooms were divided into upright lights by mullions and graced by tracery. The bigger

59. Typical windows of contrasting periods
a. wood-mullioned unglazed window, Troutbeck, Westmorland
b. stone-mullioned window, rebated for glazing, Gilcrux Grange, Cumberland
c. bow windows, Bongate, Appleby, Westmorland

windows of the late 16C and early 17C, more square in proportion, were divided into tiers of upright lights by transoms as at Cliburn Hall (W) or Pool Bank, Witherslack (L). Long, horizontal windows were divided by simple mullions; the grouping between stouter king mullions found, for instance, in the Central Pennines is uncommon in this region. The upright windows of late 17C Large Houses were divided by a single mullion and transom of stone or timber; though these usually have been replaced by later sliding sash windows the original form may be seen, e.g., at Askham Hall (W) and in a ruined house at Ullock (C). In Small Houses mullions remained in use to divide long and square windows until late in the 18C and at all levels they returned with the Gothic Revival early in the 19C.

Most medieval windows had a deep splayed moulding to mullions and jambs, though the more sophisticated hollow chamfer (concave or cavetto) may occasionally be seen. Later, about the turn of the 17C, square cut mullions and transoms were adopted and remained in use for over 80 years in houses and positions of lower and lower status, though more boldly shaped details such as the convex or ovolo mould and the double curve or cyma mould were used and, especially in the mid 18C, a sharp 45° chamfer was popular. Medieval and later mullioned windows were often set beneath a drip or label mould which provided some protection from the rain dripping from eaves which lacked any sort of gutter; in late 17C examples there was often a continuous label encompassing windows and doors. While these details were properly carved in sandstone, where this material was not available the practical and aesthetic qualities of the detail were achieved as could best be managed

---

60. Window details

A. Tall windows, medieval

a. unglazed lancet window with cusped head and interlaced iron bars

b. and **c.** elevation and cross-section of a wood-mullioned and transomed window based on an example at Glassonby (C), showing frame pegged together and diamond set wooden bars for removeable glazing (1)

d. diagram showing hinged internal shutters

B. Elongated windows, late medieval

a. alternative mouldings: cavetto or hollow chamfer (2), flat splay (3), reserved chamfer (4), ovolo (5), cyma (6)

b. and **c.** elevation and cross-section of a three-light mullioned window under a drip or label mould (7) with alternative treatments shown in each light: unglazed and with vertical iron bar (8), diamond lattice panes wired to a horizontal iron bar and set in a side hung outward opening casement (9), and later insertion of a wooden frame with a single horizontal glazing bar (10)

d. diagram showing splay and rebate to receive glazed lattice

C. Square windows, sub-medieval

a. alternative mouldings: cyma (11), cavetto (12), chamfer (13), square cut (14)

b. square window with square-cut surround and original square-cut mullion removed and replaced by fixed wooden window with small panes.

c. square window as **b.** but with horizontal sliding sash

d. diagram showing section through horizontal sliding sash

D. Tall windows, Renaissance

a. alternative mouldings: full architrave moulding (15), simplified architrave with chamfer (16), as (16) but square cut (17)

b. and **c.** elevation and cross-section of double hung, vertically sliding sashes with normal panes

d. diagram cut away to show frame and weights

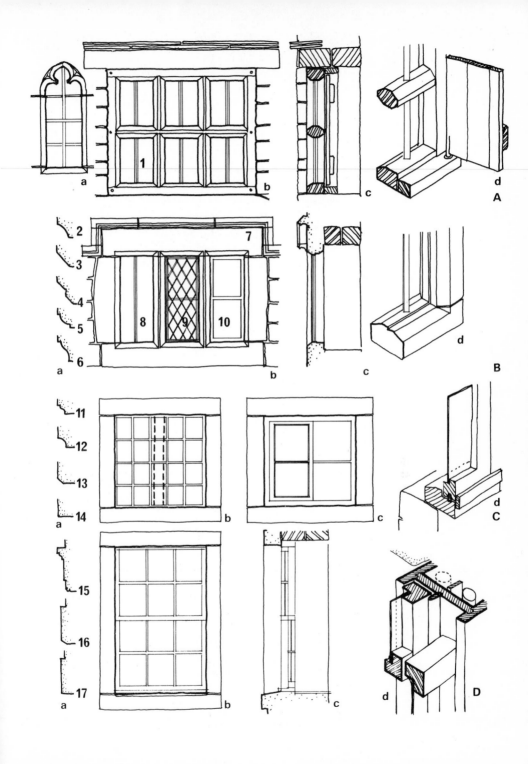

through the use of simple projecting courses of slatestone. Depressed mullions, in which the window was set back beyond a separate splayed mould, were also used at this time. Under Renaissance influence, classical architraves were introduced, at first bold or even coarse in detail, but later refined until nothing more than a simple square cut projection around head and jambs and on to the cill acknowledged this foreign influence.

Window frames and glazing techniques reflected the demands, sometimes competing, of fashion and comfort. Early medieval windows were entirely unglazed (as may be seen even as late as the heavily barred windows of Stonehouse, Naworth, C) or had glass in the upper parts and wooden shutters below. At Preston Patrick Hall (W) the sockets for the drawbar which secured the shutters were carved out of the solid stone of the mullions and jambs. Hinged shutters also survive behind the wooden mullioned and transomed windows of a house, possibly late 16C in date, at Glassonby (C). Some of the earliest surviving Small Houses retain windows consisting of a heavy squared frame with diamond-shaped wooden mullions. Lighter vertical bars in timber or wrought iron in both timber and stone windows testify to the use of lattices, presumably here as elsewhere formed of square or diamond-shaped quarries of glass set in lead cames and wired to the bars. As glazing became customary during the late 16C in Large Houses and the late 17C in Small Houses the mullions and jambs were rebated to take the lattices and side hung opening casements of wrought iron introduced. Double hung or vertically sliding sashes being used in Large Houses in the early 18C were gradually employed in Small Houses towards the end of the century; though at first the upper sash was fixed and the lower sash raised on blocks or wedges eventually the familiar counter-weighted pattern came into use. In Small Houses, especially, there was a long period in which the late mullioned windows had simple wooden window frames with side hung opening casements and in which the square windows without mullions were filled with the so-called Yorkshire sliding sash, a cheaper and simpler alternative to double-hung sashes particularly suitable for this window shape. As techniques of glass making improved so the small barely translucent quarries of spun glass gave way to the larger panes of cylinder glass and eventually to the very large panes of drawn sheet or polished plate glass of the later 19C.

In using window details as a guide to dating one should take care to note the way in which an old building may show traces of several periods as early small unglazed openings were blocked and replaced by others which in turn were modified according to each succeeding fashion; taking care also to note how contemporary windows of several types were used in the same building, the most up to date being used on the front, obsolescent types being used on the sides and rear and perhaps a completely archaic type used on a cellar or basement or an attic at the back.

Doors and doorways

Variations in design at the entrance to the vernacular houses included the shape of the doorway, the moulding of jambs, the decoration at the head, the method of hanging the door itself and its design and construction.

Early medieval doorways were usually low and wide with a pointed arch at the head, flat or hollow chamfered jambs, a drip course terminating in carved corbels. Heavy doors of alternate layers of vertical and horizontal battens pegged together were

61. Typical doorways of different periods
a. moulded jambs and decorated lintel, 1677, Lessonhall, Cumberland
b. classical architrave and cornice including false keystone, 1734, Burgh-by-Sands, Cumberland

A

B

C

hung in rebates in the stone jambs from long wrought-iron strap hinges turning on iron gudgeons set in the masonry; they were usually secured by a heavy wooden drawbar sliding into a deep recess in the wall, and where defence against attack by raiders was important then a separate inner hinged iron grille as already mentioned was provided in case the outer door was burned or battered down. In the Lake Counties such early medieval forms were retained in use well into the 16C, especially near the Scottish Border.

At the end of the 16C and during the early part of the 17C emphasis passed in Large Houses to the open doorway at the foot of a multi-storey porch. Such a doorway would have a four-centred arch with a splayed or moulded jamb. The arch would be carved out of the solid from a deep stone lintel, possibly with

---

62. Door details

A. Medieval doorways

a. doorway with two-centred arch (1), label mould (2) carried on carved corbels (3), door of two layers of planks alternately laid and pegged together (4)

b. cross-section showing cavetto or hollow chamfer mouldings
examples from Large Houses:

    c. at Yanwath (W)

    d. at Millbeck Hall (C) 1592

    e. at Upper Denton (C)

    f. at Millrigg, Culgaith (C) 1597

B. Sub-medieval doorways

g. doorway with false four-centred arch (5), label mould with returned ends (6), carved panel with raised lettering (7), door of vertical planks with cover strips and battens inside (8)

h. cross-section showing flat splay
examples from Small Houses:

    i. at Threapland (C) 1700

    j. at Shap (W) 1696

    k. at Crosby Garrett (W) 1722

    l. at Waverton (C) 1694

C. Renaissance doorways

m. doorway with architrave (10), false keystone (11), framed and panelled door in door frame (12)

n. cross-section through door head with classical mouldings
examples from Small Houses and Cottages:

    o. at Belle Vue, Carlisle (C) 1755

    p. at Gilcrux (C) 1751

    q. at Old Mawbray (C) 1772

    r. at Sebergham (C) 1769

    s. at Grinsdale (C) 1780

    t. at Kings Meaburn (W) 1777

    u. at Dalston (C) 1795

    v. at Abbeytown (C) 1826

simple decoration; above there was usually a plaque with a crest or coat of arms (not necessarily completely authentic) and a drip course embraced both plaque and lintel.

In the second half of the 17C various crude versions of classical details were used for Large Houses in embellishment of a basically medieval design or more accurately and so more convincingly as part of a considered Renaissance composition; doors at Catterlen Hall (C) and Tullie House, Carlisle (C) are examples. The typical anglo-baroque doorway had a square head beneath a broken segmental pediment; the door was surrounded by a deep bolection mould and was hinged to an inner door frame which was itself framed and panelled with bolection moulding round the six or eight panels and fitted with a lock such as those which Lady Anne Clifford was pleased to give to those who earned her favour.

From the middle of the 18C the doorway and its door based on pattern book designs had settled into a conventional form, though even within the vernacular examples great ingenuity was shown in the variation of design of architrave and panelled doorway within the accepted rules. The typical Small House of the late 17C had a doorway with a false four-centred arch, i.e., a pointed head with flat sides carved out of a deep lintel, simple jambs, a drip mould with dropped and returned ends, and possibly a set of initials and a date standing out in relief from a sunken panel on the lintel. There were many variations of the decorated lintel, one of the most popular being to carry the moulding of the jamb up and down the lintel in a battlemented effect. Another popular practice, especially in the early 18C, was to carve a religious, patriotic, or self-congratulatory motto on the lintel. The wooden door of vertical boards, cover-stripped joints and horizontal inner battens was hinged to swing into a rebate of the stone doorway.

After a brief interval about the middle of the 18C when anglo-baroque details were used for Small Houses design settled down to a simplification of the Georgian doorway with pediment, architrave, and panelled door, or an even more simple square headed doorway with a square cut or slightly chamfered set of projecting stone jambs. Variations included the use of rusticated jambs with false voussoirs carved out of a single lintel. Following the introduction late in the 18C of a lobby between the front door and staircase a fanlight was needed and provided in an arched or square head above the door and frame. The panelled door included planted mouldings and raised and fielded panels. A fairly large proportion of the Small Houses in the sandstone

128

63. Interior fittings
a. spice cupboard, dated 1681, Heaning, Windermere, Westmorland
b. bread cupboard, dated 1715, The Common, Windermere, Westmorland

areas bear dates between about 1680 and 1850 and the design variations can be fairly easily traced. In the remainder of the Lake Counties, however, the crudely formed doorway openings give little guidance, shape is constant and unremarkable, mouldings absent, and a doorway presumably dating from the late 17C shows little difference from that of 100 years later or, perhaps, from one a century earlier.

Internal ornament

The internal decoration of the Large House followed national fashion in, e.g., plasterwork or panelling, though in all houses subsequent alterations – insertion of ceilings, wall coverings, etc. – leave little original ornament to be seen. In Small Houses the most interesting period is that between 1660 and 1740 when yeoman families were either at their most prosperous or at their most confident.

The arrangement of the inglenook which dominated Small Houses of the late 17C and early 18C has already been described. The fire of peat or wood burned not in a fireplace but on a hearth stone contained in the deep recess between a wooden boarded screen and the front wall of the house. The smoke was collected in a tall hooded chimney and the inglenook was lit by a fire window. This focus of the domestic activities of the household, bearing all the traditions of the hearth, was given its share of such ornament as the yeoman could afford. The bressumer was arched and decorated with stopped mouldings; the post was moulded and given some token of significance as a 'witching post', the heck partition provided the back for a fixed bench, the opposite side of the fire was reserved for the chair, the most prestigious, sometimes the only chair in the room. The spice cupboard set in the hearth wall was given a door moulded and carved with initials and a date; during the 18C this item developed into a full height bureau with cupboard, drawers, and a desk top. As coal succeeded peat as a fuel the hearthstone and hooded chimney were replaced by a fireplace and conventional flue and the inglenook was eliminated. The fireplace was the centre of the cast iron range bearing the name of some local foundry, incorporating an oven, tank for boiling water, and a huge crane from which the heavy cast iron cauldrons and frying pan were suspended. Such a burnished and brightly black-leaded range

---

64. Interior details of Small Houses

a. cross-section of a typical two-unit or cross-passage house of late 17C/early 18C period looking towards the hearth and showing inglenook (1), hearthstone (2) with position for chair (3) and for fixed bench (4), beam over, arched and moulded on the underside (5) carried on post (6) at end of 'heck' partition, spice cupboard (7) and other 'keeping holes' let into wall, 'fire window' (8). Within the loft space is the hooded chimney (9) incorporating a 'beef box'; cantilevered beams (10) support the chimney stack (11); crane or adjustable hook (12) carries cooking pans

b. cross-section looking in the opposite direction and showing door to parlour/bedroom (or 'bower') (13), door to pantry (14), muntin and plank partition (15), three-stage dresser or 'bread cupboard' (16). Within the loft space are upper crucks (17) and an unglazed window in the gable (18), there being no chimney stack from the unheated parlour

c. alternative loft with plaster or stone hood gathered to a chimney stack placed forward to avoid interference with ridge

d. 19C cast iron range as may still be seen in the living room or kitchen with sandstone surround and projecting mantelpiece (19), firegrate (20), hinged crane for cooking utensils (21), oven (22) with adjustable draught, tank for boiling water (23)

e. typical carved door to spice cupboard

f. panelling with alternate studs and moulded planks grooved in

g. alternative panelling with laths sprung into studs and plastered

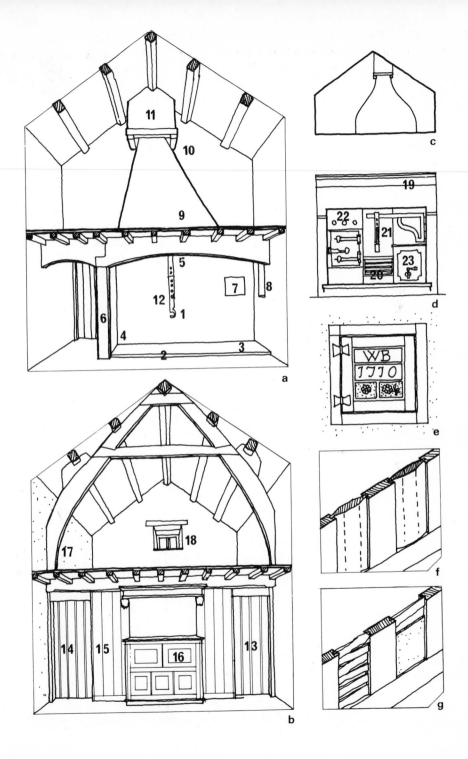

was to be seen in every Lakeland 'kitchen' until recently. At the opposite end of the principal room was a wooden partition with doors to parlour and pantry. This was made either of alternate moulded stiles and plain wooden panels or of alternate studs and plaster panels. Often a 'bread cupboard' was built into the partition, consisting of two sets of cupboards, one open-fronted, the other closed, and a projecting canopy above, all heavily carved and moulded and usually incorporating a set of initials and a date. Between there were the long rectangular table with its benches for general use and the circular drop or gate-leg table with chairs for the formal occasions.

Few of the traditional farmhouse kitchens are likely to survive. On the working farms the peat on the hearth and the coal in the grate gave way in turn during the mid-20C to the anthracite burned in the enclosed stove of 'Aga' or 'Rayburn' type. In the ordinary house central heating has meant the elimination of the fireplace altogether, or its resurrection for burning logs during the winter. Similarly, many of the cupboards and sections of panelling have fallen victim to the enthusiasm of the typical farmer's wife for paper-hanging or to the persuasiveness of the travelling antique dealer. There must be many private houses which have been lovingly restored but the ordinary visitor to the Lake Counties must rely on preserved examples as at Town End, Troutbeck (W) or collections like the Lakeland Museum of Life and Industry at Kendal (W).

For an accurate, though often incomplete, picture of the furnishing, fittings, and general air of internal ornament one must turn to probate inventories which listed, sometimes room by room, the deceased's moveable possessions. In the 17C these were comparatively few; apart from the tables, benches, and a few chairs in the 'house' there might only be a clock and the essential iron pots, hooks, spits, poker, etc. for the hearth and pewter for the table; in the 'bower' or parlour there might be a chest, a cupboard, a set of bedstocks, and the bedding; on the loft there would be one or two more beds, other chests, and bits and pieces of wood or ironwork. But the surviving evidence suggests that these few items were quite richly decorated as if the wealth and controlled ostentation which had built or rebuilt the house and adorned it with moulded doorways and mullioned windows extended also to the internal fittings. In the 18C greater prosperity for many, though not all, of the dalesmen was reflected in a greater number of items of furniture – screens, mirrors, corner cupboards to display pottery or glassware, matched tables and chairs. At the same time the more

extensive accommodation in the houses and the greater speciali-
sation in the use of rooms meant that furniture was disposed in
a way we would regard as normal rather than being mixed up
room by room. A change in taste combined with increasing skill
and improved tools on the part of the craftsmen led to a change
from the exuberant but rather crude decoration of the 17C to the
much more controlled and elegant work of the 18C and early
19C – change also from decoration vernacular in characteristics
to that more polite.

A good deal of work has still to be done on the sources of
designs for mouldings and other decorative items on the fixed
elements for the buildings as well as for the designs for furniture. Time scales show quite early introduction of some of the
fashionable details as well as their very extended use in more
and more humble situations. In some parts of the country evidence has appeared of 'factories' making stone dressings for
mullioned windows in up-to-date style, such may have existed
in the Lake Counties, providing models for other carving as well
as prefabricated items. No doubt craftsmen working on Great
Houses trained others in details which were adapted for use at
the vernacular level. Eventually the spread of pattern books and
of furniture made in the workshops such as those in Lancaster
magnified the polite and reduced the vernacular elements in
building and ornament.

Comparisons

Here are collected comparative time scales showing the use of various house plans and decorative details and generalised maps showing the distribution of the main walling and roofing materials. In conclusion the return of vernacular architecture in the more sophisticated form of the vernacular revival at the end of the 19th Century is briefly noted.

	CLASSIFICATION	DIAGRAM	1400	50	1500	50	1600	50	1700	50	1800	50
LARGE HOUSES	Tower-houses											
	Bastle houses											
	Semi-fortified											
	Non-fortified											
	Multi-storey porch											
	Anglo-baroque, Georgian, &c											

	CLASSIFICATION	DIAGRAM	1660	70	80	90	1700	10	20	30	40	1750	60	70	80	90	1800	10	20	30	40	50
SMALL HOUSES	Two-unit houses																					
	Cross-passage																					
	Continuous outshut																					
	Double pile																					
	Others																					
COTTAGES	Single storey																					
	Miniature																					
	Single-fronted																					

65. Comparative time scales of plan types

The various time scales established from dated examples for plan types have been combined here. Different scales have been used for the time span of Large Houses, which is longer than that of the other two classes. There are too few dated examples for satisfactory time scales to be established for single-storey and miniature Cottages.

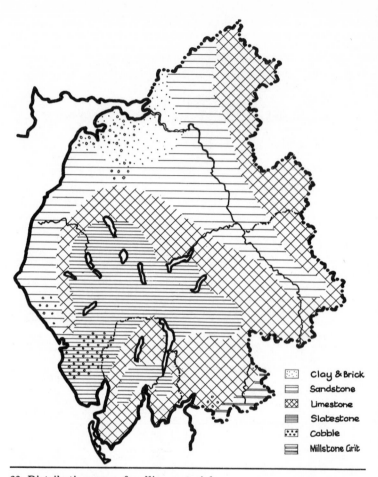

Clay & Brick
Sandstone
Limestone
Slatestone
Cobble
Millstone Grit

66. Distribution map of walling materials

The map shows the fairly precise divisions in the areas in which various materials were used, as may be seen in travelling through the region. All the materials were used simultaneously except that brick succeeded clay in northern Cumberland; it was also used with increasing frequency during the late 18C and the 19C in the Eden Valley and West Cumberland. Cobble was used a great deal in local patches, especially on the Solway Plain and in South-west Cumberland, usually as a mixture with other materials.

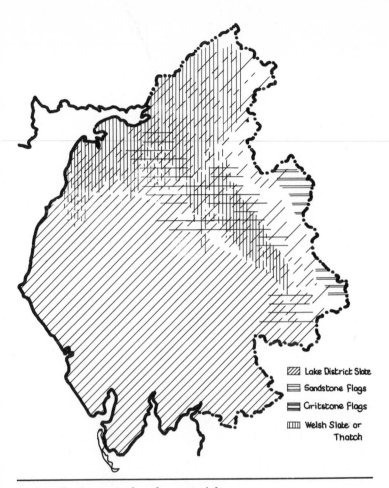

Lake District Slate
Sandstone Flags
Gritstone Flags
Welsh Slate or Thatch

67. Distribution map of roofing materials

This map is less clear than that of walling materials, as the shorter life of a roofing material leads to repair and replacement. In general, however, the widespread use of Lake District Slate is indicated, together with those portions of the Eden Valley and Solway Plain where sandstone flags are used, and the parts of the Pennine regions where flagstones of millstone grit were used. The hatching for Welsh Slate and Thatch includes the very few examples in which thatch survives, visible or concealed by corrugated roofing, and the more numerous examples where Welsh Slate has been used at a steep pitch, almost certainly as a replacement for thatch. There must have been many examples in the Lake District and the South-west in which thatch has been replaced by Lake District Slate.

68 and 69. Comparative time scales for doors and windows
A. door shape and mouldings. The time scales are based on about 250 dated doorways from Small Houses and Cottages from all parts of the region. They show, among other things, the relatively short period between the end of the use of the false arched head and its revival in the 19C, the long overlap of fashions, archaic forms remaining in use long after they have been superseded in more up-to-date buildings, the long retention of medieval influence in, e.g., the use of moulded jambs, the changeover in the 1720s from mainly medieval to mainly renaissance influence, the introduction of fanlights after about 1770 to light internal lobbies.
B. window mouldings. The time scales are based on about 220 windows which can reasonably be dated as being in buildings bearing a reliable datestone, taken from Small Houses and Cottages in all parts of the region; they show, e.g., long overlap of styles, quick introduction of new styles in up-to-date buildings, short interval before revival of medieval styles with long retention of medieval influence.
C. window shape. Time scales based on the same examples show the succeeding phases of elongated, square, and tall windows in Small Houses and Cottages, reflecting changes from low to intermediate and then to tall room heights.

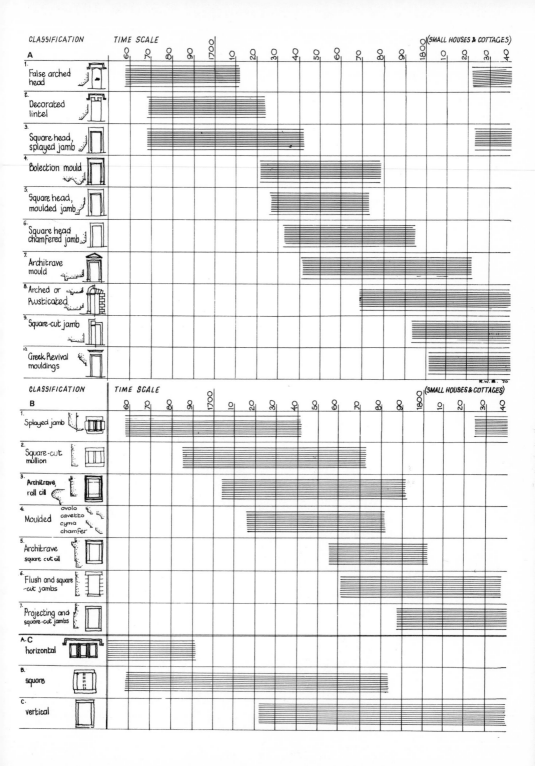

CLASSIFICATION | TIME SCALE | (SMALL HOUSES & COTTAGES)

A
1. False arched head
2. Decorated lintel
3. Square head, splayed jamb
4. Bolection mould
5. Square head, moulded jamb
6. Square head chamfered jamb
7. Architrave mould
8. Arched or Rusticated
9. Square-cut jamb
10. Greek Revival mouldings

CLASSIFICATION | TIME SCALE | (SMALL HOUSES & COTTAGES)

B
1. Splayed jamb
2. Square-cut mullion
3. Architrave, roll cill
4. Moulded — ovolo, cavetto, cyma, chamfer
5. Architrave square cut cill
6. Flush and square-cut jambs
7. Projecting and square-cut jambs

A.C horizontal
B. square
C. vertical

Conclusion
The Vernacular Revival

Towards the end of the 19C there developed a movement among some of the most influential architects of the day to seek inspiration for their designs for domestic buildings among the smaller houses, the cottages, and the farm buildings of the countryside. Design in the Gothic Revival styles had been dominated by the buildings of monumental scale; architects had attempted to reduce the scale of features borrowed from castles and cathedrals to make them suit their designs for small country houses and suburban villas rather than seeking more appropriate, vernacular, details.

Philip Webb had been a forerunner of this movement in his design for the Red House, Bexleyheath, for William Morris, using local materials and traditional forms in an informal and picturesque manner. Webb was also responsible for two houses in Brampton (C), Green Lanes and Four Gables, built 1876–8 at the time that he was designing the church of St. Martin for the Earl of Carlisle. Four Gables was built of the local sandstone with a Lake District Slate roof; with its corbelled parapet it has something of the character and much of the solidity of a tower house, but it has the compactness of an early 19C double-pile farmhouse and the splayed mullions of a late 17C Small House. Although drawing on local precedent it is clearly architect-designed.

M. H. Baillie Scott was one of the most prolific of the group and his principal local work is Blackwell at Bowness-on-Windermere (W), 1900. Here vernacular buildings provided the starting point for the design externally, but the wealth of half timbering internally and the extent of Art Nouveau decoration show that this architect diverged far from his vernacular point of origin.

C. F. A. Voysey (1857–1941) was the most influential of all the architects of the Vernacular Revival movement. A Yorkshireman brought up in London, Voysey had no local connections with the Lake Counties but several of his most significant buildings may be found there. Designs were prepared in 1898 for a house at Glassonby (C) which was not in fact built but whose

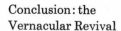

design included red sandstone walls, Lake District Slate roof, and square cut mullions among tokens of local influence. The much illustrated Broadleys, Windermere (L), has a hipped roof, dormer windows and rough cast walls. Moor Crag, Windermere (L), has the device of cross gables, label moulds, stone dressings in rendered brick walls which Voysey used frequently. The smaller Littleholme, Kendal (W), of 1909 reverted in its design to the square solid precedent of Webb's Four Gables though with a steep-pitch hipped roof, deep eaves, and no parapets. It will be clear that these designs paid very limited homage to local buildings; they could not be mistaken for another Town End, Troutbeck, let alone Yanwath Hall.

The local buildings of these national architects had some local influence, e.g., in the design of the group of cottages at Sawrey (L), but their interest lies perhaps chiefly in evidence of an attitude of mind. These designers were following romantic writers such as Thomas Hardy in finding significance in the ordinary, vernacular, buildings of untutored countrymen, using simple direct means to solve simple functional problems, using local materials in a direct, unsophisticated manner, adapting architectural decoration to simple needs of emphasis and punctuation, emphasising, as Voysey did, the national identity of his architecture and the regional or local or vernacular components which made up that national identity.

The vernacular Revival phase followed close on the loss of virtually all vernacular qualities in domestic buildings erected in the Lake Counties. Thus one long phase of architectural development ended as another, hopefully stressing regional characteristics, began and is still in progress.

Suggestions for further work

A field handbook such as this cannot pretend to be definitive but must rather be regarded as a summary of certain broad generalisations which appear valid on present information and a guide to the further work which can help to test these generalisations in various localities and to continue the study to a greater and greater depth. In the *Illustrated Handbook of Vernacular Architecture* three techniques of study of vernacular buildings were briefly outlined: those of extensive recording with the aid of a checklist, intensive recording by means of measured drawing, and collection of documentary information to illuminate the mysteries revealed by the other two techniques. All three procedures may well be applied to further study of the vernacular buildings of the Lake Counties. Examples of what can be done include the following:

a. Village or parish studies: a selected district can be covered by means of an extensive survey, significant buildings selected from the results of the survey and given intensive study, and records such as tithe maps checked to fill gaps revealed by the field work.

b. Farmstead surveys: the same procedure can be adopted for the farm buildings, again, extensive surveys providing the information from which significant farmsteads may be selected for intensive study, amplified by study of farm account books, sale particulars, etc.

c. Building type studies: one building type, e.g., the miner's cottage, the water mill, the lime kiln, etc., may be selected; extensive survey over wide parts of a defined district can reveal distributions; known, and preferably threatened, examples may be measured and photographed, the results again compared to firms' account books or estate surveys.

d. Building material surveys: although there is greater homogeneity in use of building materials in this region than in some others, nevertheless there is appreciable local variety to be detected in some parts of the region. Extensive surveys can be made to give more accurate distribution maps than are possible in this handbook.

e. Surveys of constructional methods: since so many houses are being altered, and some demolished, at the present time, conditions are ideal for study of constructional methods such as those which have been long established in study of cruck construction.

f. Architectural detail surveys: further time scales may be prepared for door and window details, types of decorative plaque, changes in panelling or in use of furniture; again the widespread alterations make the present an ideal time – perhaps the last possible time.

g. Studies of urban vernacular architecture: here perhaps is the most urgent task. Control of development in the countryside and the strong demand for buildings which are preserved through conversion acts as a limit to the loss of evidence of vernacular building practices. In the towns the situation is rather different; demands for commercial redevelopment, need for new roads, for car parks, etc., and the unsuitability of many old shops or houses or industrial buildings for any contemporary use mean that demolition must continue apace. It is essential that these minor buildings which make up the major part of the towns of the region should be studied and their characteristics recorded if knowledge of their former existence is to be handed down.

If this little handbook serves to help residents, tourists, students, and other visitors to the Lake Counties to an increased awareness of the wealth of vernacular architecture which still survives and a greater understanding of its characteristics, then its preparation will have been worth-while.

Vernacular Trail 1

71. Troutbeck,
Westmorland

One of the most popular villages among visitors to Lakeland is Troutbeck, Westmorland. It consists of a series of hamlets and clusters of
farms (many now converted for holiday and retirement use) strung
along a road which is itself simply the tarmac portion of a braided series
of tracks, joining, parting and rejoining each other in a roughly north–
south direction. There is no major crossroads, no natural focus, no
dominating hamlet; the church is nearly half a mile away in the bottom
of the valley and so there is no centre and little sense of nucleation in the
village. Fortunately the main road between Windermere and Penrith
via Kirkstone Pass avoids the village, meeting it only at the north end,
Town Head, and so one may walk and linger through the village from
cluster to cluster.

The village spreads along a series of springs which may still be seen as
St. John's Well, St. Margaret's Well, etc., on the roadside. The farms
are located along the slope of the valley, equally accessible from the
steep fell land above and the only slightly less steep arable and meadow
land below. Across the valley there are plain signs of the pack horse
track and drovers' road to Kentmere, Longsleddale and Shap, crossing
hills which the modern roads avoid. There is no manor house, though
Town End, the National Trust property and headquarters of the Browne
family of yeomen, is rather larger than the other houses. The villagers
evidently depended on a difficult agriculture on the inhospitable land
until slate quarrying brought prosperity in the mid 18C and provided in
quarry waste building materials for many of the houses and barns. In the
middle of the 19C, visitors came in numbers which had been multiplied
by the arrival of the railway at Windermere in 1847; the two inns were
rebuilt, new houses were built for Manchester merchants, and Trout-

beck acquired the appearance which it substantially retains. Perhaps

because of these later developments the simple plans of the earlier houses have been obscured in alteration and extension.

A route has been assumed from south to north, starting on the Ambleside road and finishing at the junction with the main road south of Town Head. All the houses have slatestone walls and Lake District Slate roofs, and some of the interesting items which can be seen from the road are mentioned.

1. On l.h.s., Small House, *Kilns*, end on to slope, modified two-unit plan, incorporates date 1700.

2. On r.h.s. one looks down upon *Town End House*, a 17C building, facing SE, to which is attached a late 19C double-pile house facing NE, and with an L-shaped block of farm buildings enclosing the yard. There is also a variant bank barn running deep into the hillside. A little further S is

3. *Town Foot* which the RCHM notes as having inside a cupboard dated 1694, and bearing the initials G and A.B.

4. Further N of Town End House is *Town End Farm*, facing S with plaque 1611 *WB*. The L-shaped house is in parallel with the combination farm buildings.

5. At the road junction there is on the l.h.s. *Town End*, the most important house in the village, belonging to the National Trust and open at stated times to visitors. The house is now rendered and whitewashed, has rather a complicated plan as a result of various additions, has tall, very prominent, cylindrical chimneys, two being on corbelled projections from gabled walls. The windows are generally modernized though several wood-mullioned windows may be seen including one with transoms lighting a staircase. There is a reset stone GB 1626. Inside there are many original items of wood work including dates of 1670, 1672, 1687, and 1702.

6. Opposite, on r.h.s. is the *Barn*, a bank barn with two deep projecting wings and the canopy over the barn doors extended as a gallery. There are several unglazed mullioned windows, possibly re-used from a house; over one are the initials G and E B 1666. The cart house extension on the north uses part of a cruck blade as a lintel.

7. Further on the r.h.s., partly hidden behind an L-shaped barn, there is a derelict house which probably faced SE across the valley so that we see the rear including a two-storey wing with projecting chimney breast and stack and a two-storey porch with an open doorway, wide, and with what appears to be part of a cruck blade as the arched lintel. Among the blocked windows there are also several with thin wooden mullions and vertical bars for the glass lattices.

8. Next to this, on r.h.s., is *Low House*, notable for its corbelled chimney stacks on the cross wings; one bears the date 1627 and the other 1811. The roof of the main block is extended between the wings to form a gallery.

9. Up a lane to the left is *Robin Lane Cottage*, modernized but with a central chimney base with a cylindrical stack and the date 1626 GB.

10. Opposite the *Institute* (1869) is *North Fold*, at the junction of the road which drops down to the bridge and the church. The larger, and probably older, wing of the L-shaped house includes a five-light oriel window projecting from the first floor on short timber cantilevers and with wood splayed mullion windows now blocked with slate. The rather

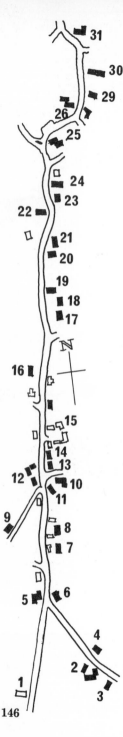

later wing facing SE has, according to the RCHM, a cupboard dated 1674. At the opposite end there is a granary extension with an external stair and the lower part curiously chamfered off for ease of access.

11. A *bank barn* of rough quarry waste showing the typical angular cleavage has a wing with a 'spinning gallery' at the first floor.

12. Opposite the road junction, on the l.h.s., is *Brow Head*, a house and bank barn. The house displays a diamond-shaped plaque T and M B 1692; on the southern gable the tapered cylindrical stack is raised on a base which is cantilevered on short wooden beams. Inside, the RCHM records a cupboard with the same date. The whitewashed walls have modern windows, the lower range breaking a continuous drip course.

The bank barn has the date 1868 roughly inscribed on a stone over the winnowing door. Other features include the continuous canopy at the lower level carried on timber brackets, the continuous drip course at the junction with the main wall, the tall thin quoins of slatestone and the unusual square ventilators, perhaps acting as a dovecot, under the eaves.

13. On the r.h.s., opposite Brow Head, a cottage has been made out of a bank barn whose cantilevered canopy and the straight joint of the barn door survive.

14. Further along, at a bend in the road, one passes the back of a house two rooms deep with a landing window showing the position of the staircase and the porch locating the door. This, like so many houses in Troutbeck, really faces SE, across the valley and away from the road. However, the house has been altered and it is doubtful, for instance, if the cylindrical chimney stacks are entirely original.

15. On the r.h.s. a group of buildings at *High Fold* includes a barn at right angles to the slope, High Fold itself, an L-shaped house with a cupboard dated 1689, a late-19C double-pile Small House built of neat slatestone, a bank barn of the same material with crow-stepped gables. Facing south there is a two-unit house with an attached granary, while on the l.h.s. of the road a later house completes this little enclosure.

16. On the l.h.s. a track leads to the altered houses of the Crag, and, high on the slope, behind Crag House, one can see the ivy-clad ruin of a Small House including two four-light and one five-light windows with rather slender wooden mullions and vertical iron bars for glazing.

17. There is a gap before another little group appears at Longmire Yeat. One Small House, *Stoneythwaite*, has a projecting chimney stack in a gable but with a window immediately below.

18. The adjacent house, *Longmire Yeat* itself, includes an inscribed stone in the gable chimney stack GB 1649 with slate water tabling. The windows have been altered, though probably in their original positions. The door has a rough pediment of projecting slates.

19. At right angles there is a *house* of well-finished slatestone with a limestone plaque dated 1879 and a thin slate roof with deep projecting eaves and a barge boarded verge. The tall rooms, tall windows, and tall panes of glass contrast with the low horizontal lines of Longmire Yeat.

20. Further along the r.h.s. there is a *barn* at right angles to the slope and a late-19C double-pile *house*. The barn incorporates a wood-mullioned window with an elbowed wooden lintel.

21. Next on the r.h.s., almost opposite Great House and St. Margaret's Well, there is a long *barn* with an extension at the north end and a hipped roof – a very unusual feature in Troutbeck – at the other end.

The barn door has a cantilevered canopy and is in the centre of what appears to be a five- or seven-bay barn; there are two rows of slit ventilators over a continuous slate drip course. Below the barn level there are cow houses, etc., including an arched door in the southern gable. The chimney stack is a puzzling feature in a barn!

22. On the l.h.s., below a reduced Great House, there is a variant bank barn running across the slope; tall barn doors open on each side, there is access to the cow house through the gable and there is an outshut on the northern side.

23. On the r.h.s. the house *Drummermire* has a spice cupboard dated 1686 WB according to the RCHM.

24. At this point one looks down upon the curiously named *Jownie Wife House*, a range of buildings including a barn, etc., cut into the slope, a two-unit house facing south, and a granary apparently added to the house down the slope and now taken into the dwelling. Interesting points include the projecting canopy and cheeks of the barn door, the crude drip courses above the renewed windows, the chimney stack forward of the ridge, and, at the rear, the semi-circular staircase bulge.

25. The Mortal Man Inn, rebuilt in the late 19C, incorporates some late-17C features.

26. From alongside the Inn one may see the group at *High Green*, including *Beckside*, a modernised house with a large plaster panel W and IB 1686 and a canopied bank barn with limestone quoins, a glazed-in winnowing door, and a dated plaque 1890.

27. Alongside there is a whitewashed house, possibly converted from a barn and with a projecting covered gallery.

28. A little further north there is a house with a continuous outshut and lines of projecting through stones in the gable.

29. Still further to the north there is a late-19C *bank barn* with a continuous canopy at the lower level. Behind there is a Small House whitewashed, with later windows but continuous label moulds, a projecting wing at the rear and a range of farm buildings attached.

30, 31. Further houses of the Town Head hamlet may be seen as the village ends in the main road to Kirkstone Pass.

References

J. D. Marshall, *Old Lakeland*, David & Charles, Newton Abbot, 1971. Chapter Six is devoted to Troutbeck.

Royal Commission on Historical Monuments (England), *Inventory for Westmorland*, London, 1936, pp. 227–9 with map.

S. H. Scott, *A Westmorland Village*, London, 1904.

James Walton, 'Lake District Homesteads' in *Country Life*, 24 Oct. 1952, pp. 1319–22.

73. Milburn, Westmorland

Milburn is probably the most perfect example of the line of nucleated villages which runs along the 600 ft. contour at the foot of the Pennine escarpment from Castle Carrock in Cumberland south into Stainmore. In Milburn the houses form an almost continuously built-up frontage facing a broad rectangular green, and broken by narrow paths giving access to the remaining sets of farm buildings and so to an overgrown and partly abandoned circuit of back lanes. Around the village, and especially on the N and E, one may still see the long narrow fields with hedges rather than stone walls assembled out of groups of strips in the old open townfields. The narrow fellside road from Skirwith and Blencarn to Long Marton and Appleby runs beyond the southern end of the green, and without any through traffic the proportions of the green and the qualities of vernacular architecture can be appreciated without interruption.

As with several other such villages the parish church is some distance from the green and beside a river. Dedicated to St. Cuthbert, the church was in fact a chapel of Kirkby Thore, first recorded in 1227, but probably incorporating an older building. The principal house, Howgill Castle, of the Lancaster family is also outside the village, and is a much altered fortified house, with two towers and immensely thick walls, in a lonely position on the fellside. Milburn was a relatively rich village, no doubt closely packed with houses from an early date, but not only are there no survivors of the medieval peasant houses, but there is scarcely any remnant of the 17C houses which succeeded these flimsy dwellings in most parishes of the region. Instead there are many mid- and late-18C houses and even more which testify to a 19C rebuilding.

It has been suggested that the farmhouses made a sort of wall around the village green and that, on hearing of a raid, the farmers could drive

149

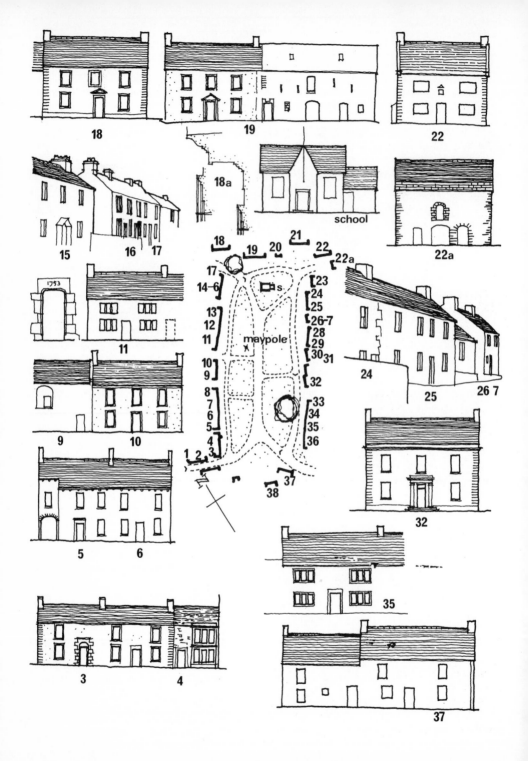

18

19

22

15 16 17

18a

school

22a

22a

11

1753

9 10

5 6

18 21 22
19 20 22a
17
14-6 23
24
13 25
12 26-7
11 28
29
10 30 31
9
32
8
7 33
6 34
5 35
4 36
1 2 3
37
38

s.

maypole

24

25 26 7

32

35

3 4

37

their cattle on to the green, block up the narrow gaps between the buildings, and so defend the village as if behind the wall. As all the existing houses were built centuries after the last Scottish raid they can give no evidence in favour of this suggestion. However, another idea, that the gaps were blocked in winter time and the green used as one large grazing and exercise yard, seems more reasonable.

The following 'trail' is described assuming the visitor enters at the south-west corner of a green which rises at right angles to the slope and so from south-west to north-east.

1, 2. Just before entering the village green there is a mid- or late-19C house, double-pile plan, with farm buildings which include a horse engine house, apsidal, at the rear.

3. Next, and facing the green, there is a farmhouse, now a Cottage and Small House, with late 19C stone dressings, but one room deep with a continuous outshut, probably converted from a cross-passage plan; stuccoed front elevation, quoins stressed.

4. Attached there is a cottage with big projecting late-19C bay windows.

5, 6. After a covered way there are two very tall late-19C houses, rough-cast, and with Welsh Slate roofs.

7. Next there is a conventional barn and stable in coursed sandstone.

8. Attached there is a double-pile house with new windows and door and rendered and pebble-dashed.

9. After a gap there is a bank barn (now the Post Office) with arched doorways to the cow-house and stable. Above there is a blocked barn door with a winnowing door inserted as if originally full-size doors were to be used to provide draught, though they would have been difficult to control at that height. The barn is of red sandstone rubble, has prominent kneelers, and the curious termination of the voussoirs at the impost found quite often in the district.

10. Attached to the bank barn there is a later-19C double-pile Small House with recent stucco.

11. There is a gap and then a farmhouse with a main elevation of dressed coursed rubble, almost of ashlar quality, square-cut mullioned windows and a decorated door lintel dated 1753. Although the position appears reasonable in a house one room deep with outshuts, local information is that the door was moved to its present position.

12. Attached there is a conventional barn and cow-house which runs into

13. A late-19C double-pile house whose red sandstone main elevation is in snecked rubble.

14. The next house, double-pile plan, has herringbone chiselling on its worked masonry.

15. An early-19C house has an ashlar front and a rubble gable.

16. A cottage and house of squared dressed rubble, one room deep with outshuts, might be adapted from a cross-passage house.

17. Attached to the last building is a late-19C double-pile house with a Welsh Slate roof. The farm building at the end has been altered. This forms the end of the north-western side of the village green.

18. Facing SW there is a Small House, one room deep with outshuts, a Welsh Slate roof, window frames with thick glazing bars and small panes probably original, set in crisp architraves, and with an architrave and pediment around the door (18a). This is placed off-centre as is customary, but not underneath the centre window, which is unusual. A barn and service rooms are attached to the house.

19. After a gap there is an interesting group which faces straight down the village green. It consists of a house and bank barn which have probably been fashioned out of a much earlier longhouse. The present house, whitewashed and with a Lake District Slate roof, appears to be one-room deep with outshuts. The attached bank barn has a corrugated iron roof over rubble walls which show signs of heightened eaves and altered openings. At the junction between house and barn there is a doorway with castellated lintel of late-17C form and indications of a blocked fire window, suggesting that the present house was built on the site of the original farm buildings and the present bank barn has been imposed on the shell of the original house.

20. Next to a timber and asbestos chalet there is a bank barn with

21. Two-storey cottage attached, and prominent kneelers.

22. The last house facing SW has a Welsh Slate roof between raking gable copings over a red sandstone wall with projecting quoins and windows which formerly had square-cut mullions. The plaque over the front door has lost its initials and date. There is a projection from the gable wall which is presumably an oven, a common feature elsewhere but uncommon in this district.

22a. At right angles and facing the back lane there is a compact bank barn bearing a date 1841 over the winnowing door.

b. On the village green is the school now closed.

23. The first house along the other side of the green is a mid-19C double-pile house, stucco on elevation but with prominent quoins and other dressings and with Greek Revival details to the doorway.

24. After a gap there is a minute one-room-up one-room-down cottage with walls of flint-like rubble attached to

25. A double-fronted house, one-room deep but with an extra bay at one end and attached to a barn which has now been converted into an antique store. These houses have early rain-water gutters carried on corbels.

26, 27. Beyond a narrow gap there is a reflected pair of tall double-pile single-fronted late-19C cottages. They have a stucco elevation with sandstone dressings including a strip pilaster quoin. One doorway has been removed as the cottages have been converted into one house.

28. There is a gap and then a late-19C double-pile house of rock-faced snecked rubble. The lower part of the roof has Lake District Slate but the upper part has Welsh slate.

29. After an arched opening there is a set of farm buildings converted into a house; the sandstone flag roof appears to have been renewed.

30. Attached to this there is a mid-19C double-pile house with white-painted stucco on the main elevation and painted stone dressings, Welsh Slate roof, and a classical doorway surround.

31. After a gap there is a house which appears to back on to the green. The red sandstone walls have what appear to be limestone bonding stones making a chequered pattern. The windows have square-cut mullions and there is a Lake District Slate roof between copings.

32. The next group consists of Milburn House, the largest in the village, with an extensive range of farm buildings including a horse engine house. The house has been renewed after a fire and is basically of double-pile plan with stucco walls, sandstone dressings, and Greek Revival details including a Doric porch.

33. Another house which appears to back on to the village green has a double-pile plan with a service wing at one end. The walls are of good quality squared rubble and there are square-cut mullions to some of the windows.

34. Attached there is a house recently modernised with coursed sand-stone rubble walls, square-cut mullioned windows, Lake District Slate roof. It is one-room deep and has an arched wooden beam, possibly a re-used cruck blade, over the entrance to the farmyard.

35. A small House, of two-unit plan, pebble dashed, has a roof with an eaves course of sandstone flags and slate above, possibly replacing thatch. The deeply worn door jamb testifies to many years of knife sharpening!

36. This row of four houses is terminated by a late-19C double-pile house with prominent bay windows. In spite of the apparent late date of this house the front door is still placed off centre

37. Around the corner and facing up the village green is a pair of cottages which, to judge from the relative positions of one of the door-ways and a chimney stack, may have been formed out of a cross-passage house

38. After noting the Wesleyan Chapel, dated 1834, and a cottage set back from the road, the route around the village green has been completed.

References

M. Beresford and J. K. St. Joseph, *Medieval England*, Cambridge, 1958, pp. 149–51, with aerial photograph.

W. Goodchild, 'Milburn, Archaeological Notes', *CW2*, Vol. 32, 1932, pp. 107–15, with sketch plan.

T. Sharp, *The Anatomy of the Village*, Penguin Books, Harmondsworth, 1946, p. 17 with plan.

Notes, references and suggestions for further study

1. The Region and its Study

a. General bibliography: the major part of the region is covered by the *Bibliography of the History and Topography of Cumberland and Westmorland*, compiled by Henry W. Hodgson and published by the Joint Archive Committee, Carlisle, 1968.

b. The *Transactions of the Cumberland and Westmorland Antiquarian and Archaeological Society*, Old Series Vols. I to XVII, 1866 to 1900, and new Series, Vol. I to date, 1901 to the present day, cover Lancashire north of the Sands as well as the other two counties, and are cited as *CW1* and *CW2* respectively here. They contain many articles about individual houses, mainly Large Houses, as well as much background material on families, agrarian history, folk customs, etc. No comprehensive index has yet been published, but most of the individual volumes have an index and in any case references to specific houses in Cumberland and Westmorland may be traced through the *Bibliography* noted above.

c. For social and economic history, the basic works are C. M. L. Bouch, *Prelates and People of the Lake Counties*, published in Kendal, 1948, and *The Lake Counties 1500–1830* by C. M. L. Bouch and G. P. Jones, Manchester, 1961. W. G. Collingwood's *Lake District History*, Kendal, 1925, is still very useful, but several more general or more popular works have recently been published, e.g., M. Lefebure, *Cumberland Heritage*, 1970; W. A. Rollinson, *A History of Man in the Lake District*, and J. D. Marshall, *Old Lakeland*, 1971.

d. A basic historical source continues to be *The History and Antiquities of the Counties of Cumberland and Westmorland*, by J. Nicolson and R. Burn, published in 1777, which had a general survey followed by accounts parish by parish. This method was followed in W. Hutchinson, *History and Antiquities of Cumberland*, 1794, including parish notes expanded by J. Housman in his *Topographical Description of Cumberland, Westmorland, Lancashire, and a part of the West Riding of Yorkshire*, 1800; and in D. and S. L. Lysons, *Magna Brittania*, Vol. 4, *Cumberland* of 1816. The parish entries vary in usefulness but the best give particulars of building materials, fuel, etc. The most useful directories (sometimes copying each other) are F. Jollie, *Jollie's Cumberland Guide and Directory*, published in Carlisle in 1811; W. Parson and W. White, *History, Directory and Gazetteer of Cumberland, Westmorland, and Furness*, Leeds, 1829; and Mannix and Whellan, *History, Gazetteer and Directory of Cumberland*, 1847, together with Mannex, *History, Topography, and Directory of Westmorland and Lonsdale North of the Sands*, 1849. Of the Victoria County Histories, two volumes for Cumberland were published in 1905 and the volumes for Lancashire include some relevant material.

e. There is a very useful summary of settlement and land utilisation, including the influence of climate, topography and geology, in parts 49 and 50 of *The Land of Britain*, the Report of the Land Utilisation Survey of Britain, ed. L. Dudley Stamp, these parts published in 1943. Among the several works and articles about local farming practices may be mentioned T. H. Bainbridge, 'Eighteenth Century Agriculture in Cumberland' in *CW2*, Vol. XLII, 1942; W. Dickinson, 'Prize Essay on the farming of Cumberland,' *Journal of the Royal Agricultural Society of England*, Vol. XIII, 1853; R. S. Dilley, 'Some words used in the agrarian history of Cumberland,' *CW2*, Vol. LXX, 1970; G. Elliott, 'The system of cultivation and evidence of enclosure in the Cumberland open fields in the Sixteenth Century,' *CW2*, LXIX, 1959; F. W. Garnett, *Westmorland Agriculture 1800–1900*, published in Kendal, 1912; E. Hughes, *North Country Life in the Eighteenth Century*, Vol. II, Cumberland and Westmorland, 1965 (mainly about the western part of Lakeland); G. P. Jones, 'The Decline of the Yeomanry in the Lake Counties,' *CW2*, Vol. LXII, 1962; C. Webster, 'Prize Essay on farming in Westmorland,' *Journal RASE*, 1868.

f. The developing interest in the scenery of the Lake District, including its vernacular architecture, is covered in E. W. Hodge, *Enjoying the Lakes*, 1957. Among the earliest accounts written for the visitor are James Clarke, *A Survey of the Lakes*, 2nd ed. 1789, and W. Wordsworth, *A Guide through the District of the Lakes . . .*, 5th ed. 1835 (latest edition 1951).

g. The few works written specifically about the architecture of the Lake Counties or even parts of the region are mentioned in notes to subsequent chapters, but here should be mentioned (Sir) Nikolaus Pevsner, *The Buildings of England: Cumberland and Westmorland*, 1967, and *North Lancashire*, 1969 (both with introductory notes on building materials by Alec Clifton-Taylor); and the invaluable *Inventory of the Historical Monuments in Westmorland*, of the Royal Commission on Historical Monuments, England, 1936, which deals with buildings whose date is ascribed to a period before 1715. Among unpublished theses at Manchester University are J. E. Partington, *Traditional Domestic Architecture of North Lancashire*, 1948, and *Traditional Domestic Architecture of the Lake District*, 1961, together with my own *Traditional Domestic Architecture of the Eden Valley*, 1952, and . . . *the Solway Plain*, 1963.

h. For general references on vernacular architecture, setting the Lake Counties in the national context, see, e.g., my *Illustrated Handbook of Vernacular Architecture*, 1970; and A. Clifton-Taylor, *The Pattern of English Building*, revised ed. 1971.

i. In the text Cumberland, Westmorland and Lancashire may be noted as (C), (W), and (L) respectively.

j. Room names have generally been given in modern terms. The variety of terms used in the past may be seen in Ch. 2 of J. D. Marshall, *Old Lakeland*, 1971.

k. As the drawings are meant to be diagrammatic, rather than measured drawings of actual examples, no scales are given, though relative size will be clear from doors, windows, etc.

a. For the fortified and semi-fortified houses the basic work remains J. C. Curwen, *The Castles and Fortified Towers of Cumberland, Westmorland and Lancashire North of the Sands*, published originally as

2. Large Houses

Notes, references and suggestions for further study	Extra Series Vol. XIII, by the Cumberland and Westmorland Antiq. and Arch. Soc. in 1913 but reproduced as a xerox edition by the Society in 1965. Useful also is the section by H. L. Honeyman in *The Three Northern Counties of England*, edited by Sir Cuthbert Headlam, 1939.

b. For some clarification of the term 'peel' or 'pele', see G. Neilson, 'Peel, its meaning and derivation,' in *Transac. Galloway Arch. Soc.*, 1894. Although about Northumberland, the transcription by C. J. Bates of 'View of the Castles, Towers, Barmekyns, Fortresses of the Frontier of the East and Middle Marches drawn up by Sir Robert Bowes and Sir Ralph Elleker at the end of the year 1541' is very useful as a guide to the use and purposes of fortified houses; it was published in *Archaeologia Aeliana* in 1891. Also useful are the plans and descriptions in R. Hugill, *Borderland Castles and Peles*, c. 1960.

c. An account and inventory of the bastles of Cumberland is included in H. G. Ramm, R. W. McDowall, and E. Mercer, *Shielings and Bastles*, prepared for the RCHM (England), 1970.

d. Many Large Houses, both fortified and non-fortified, are illustrated in W. T. McIntire and J. H. Palmer, *Historic Farmhouses in and around Westmorland*, 1946; and also in M. W. Taylor, *The Old Manorial Halls of Westmorland and Cumberland*, Extra Series, Vol. VIII, 1892, of the Cumberland and Westmorland Antiq. and Arch. Soc.

e. As already mentioned there are many articles about the Large Houses in the *Transactions* of the local Archaeological Society, and also brief but useful descriptions of them in the accounts of excursions which appear near the end of each volume.

3. Small Houses

a. Accounts with plans of small houses and references to documentary sources may be found in R. W. Brunskill, 'The Development of the Small House in the Eden Valley from 1650 to 1840', *CW2*, Vol. LIII, 1953; and 'The Clay Houses of Cumberland', *Transactions of the Ancient Monuments Society*, N.S., Vol. 10, 1962; H. S. Cowper, *Hawkshead, its History, Archaeology etc.*, 1899; P. Dixon, 'Paddock Hole: A Cumberland House with a lower end parlour,' *CW2*, Vol. LXXI, 1971; K. Hodgson, C. M. L. Bouch and C. G. Bulman, 'Lamonby Farm; a clay house at Burgh,' *CW2*, Vol. LIII, 1953; R. McDowall, 'The Westmorland Vernacular' in *Studies in Architectural History*, W. A. Singleton ed., 1956; J. D. Marshall, *Old Lakeland*, 1971; J. Walton, 'Lake District Homesteads,' *Country Life*, 1952, p. 1319; and W. M. Williams, 'The farmhouses of South-West Cumberland: a preliminary survey,' *CW2*, Vol. LIV, 1954.

b. There are many plans in the excellent thesis by N. Birdsall on Traditional Domestic Architecture of the Martindale Valley of Westmorland held in the Library of the Royal Institute of British Architects.

c. Descriptions of Small Houses with local terms and some indication of the uses of the various parts appear in James Clarke, *Survey of the Lakes*; Rev. Mr. Dodgson, *Westmorland as it was* (n.d. but c. 1825); and J. Bailey and G. Culley, *General View of the Agriculture of Cumberland*, 1793. For the type of plan considered appropriate for a local farmhouse in the mid 18C see Daniel Garret, *Designs and Estimates of farmhouses . . .*, 1747.

d. Some indication of the sort of furniture and equipment to be found in the Small Houses may be gained from, e.g., H. S. Cowper, 'Illustrations of old fashioned and obsolete contrivances in Lakeland,' *CW1*, Vol. XV,

1898, and XIII, 1895, and his *Hawkshead*; and also J. H. Martindale 'Toast Dogs, frying pans and peats,' in *CW1*, XIII, 1895.

e. The value of probate inventories in establishing the names, position, and uses of rooms in Large Houses and Small Houses, especially of the 17C and 18C, has long been recognised. In his book *Old Lakeland*, J. D. Marshall gives examples of the sort of information which may be obtained, and shows how sometimes an inventory and a surviving house may be matched. Individuals and groups can perform a rewarding task in extracting information from the inventories which are now coming into the local record offices. As an exercise before encountering the difficulties of collecting and transcribing the actual documents readers may care to work on the following selection printed in various volumes of the *Transactions* of the local Archaeological Society, and covering a range of districts, periods, and social levels:

CW1, Vol. XI, 1890, p. 32, Hawkshead, Kendal, etc., Rowland Nicholson 1590, Allan Nicholson 1616, Allan Nicholson 1663, Samuel Sandys 1683, George Nicholson 1686.

CW1, Vol. XI, pt. 2, 1891, p. 394, Edward Benson of Blackbeck 1673, John Fell of Ulverston 1688.

CW2, Vol. XL, 1940, p. 87, John Lowther 1619, W. Lowther 1695, both of Gt. Orton.

CW2, Vol. XLIX, 1959, p. 137, C. Richmond, Catterlen Hall.

CW2, Vol. XL, 1960, p. 92, College of Priests at Greystoke, 1546 survey.

CW2, Vol. LXV, 1965, p. 353, Robert Routledge of Cumcrook, Bewcastle, 1724.

CW2, Vol. LXVIII, 1967, p. 93, Five Bewcastle Wills, 1587–1617.

CW2, Vol. LXVIII, 1968, p. 183, James Brown, Stapleton, 1762.

4. Cottages

a. Some indication of what was considered adequate accommodation for cottages in the mid 18C may be gleaned from proposals for a model village at Lowther (W); see R. W. Brunskill, 'Lowther Village and Robert Adam,' *Transac. Ancient Monument Soc.*, N.S., Vol. 14, 1966-7.

b. Evidence of the death of vernacular traditions in designs for cottages may be seen in A. Harris, 'Millom, a Victorian New Town,' *CW2*, Vol. LXVI, 1966, and 'Askam Iron, the Development of Askam in Furness,' *CW2*, Vol. LXV, 1965.

5. Farm buildings

a. Reference to the farming methods and agricultural developments which formed a background to the design of farm buildings have already been suggested in the notes to Chapter 1. National developments may be understood by reference to N. Harvey, *A History of Farm Buildings*, 1970, and to designs for model farms illustrated, e.g., in J. C. Loudon, *The Encyclopedia of Agriculture*, 1842, and J. Bailey Denton, *The Farm Homesteads of England*, 1845.

b. Plans and further notes on farmbuildings may be seen in R. W. Brunskill, Neale Bursary Report, 1965, and the Thesis of N. Birdsall already quoted; both are held in the Library of the RIBA.

c. The distribution maps for bank barns are based on some 400 examples noted over the past 8 years and including 45 recorded by T. K. Eland in a dissertation held at the School of Architecture, Manchester University. The type was described and illustrated by James Walton in an article 'Upland Houses', *Antiquity*, Vol. XXX, 1956, following on an article by him, 'Lake District Homesteads,' *Country Life*, 24 Oct. 1952, p. 1319, in which he also mentioned the so-called 'spinning galleries' sometimes associated with such buildings. I owe to N. Birdsall the reference to Nettleslack, Martindale. Comparable American material includes A. L. Shoemaker, ed., *The Pennsylvanian Barn*, Kutztown, 1959; C. H. Dornbusch and J. K. Heyl, *Pennsylvania German Barns*, Allentown, 1958; and H. H. Glassie, *Pattern in the Material Folk Culture of the Eastern U.S.*, Philadelphia, 1969.

d. For horse engines the basic reference is F. Atkinson, 'The horse as a source of rotary power,' *Transac. Newcomen Society*, Vol. 33, 1960–1.

e. For laithe houses in the Pennines, see C. F. Stell, 'Pennine Houses; an Introduction,' *Folk Life*, Vol. III, 1965.

6. Urban buildings

a. For an account of Appleby as a medieval new town, see W. D. Simpson, 'The town and castle of Appleby,' *CW2*, Vol. XLIX, 1949; and M. W. Beresford, *New Towns of the Middle Ages*, 1967. Some notes on control of building development appear in C. M. L. Bouch, 'Local Government in Appleby,' CW2, Vol. LI, 1951. See also M. W. Holdgate, *A History of Appleby*, 1956. In the hearth tax returns for 1669–72, printed in J. F. Curwen, *Later Records of North Westmorland*, 1932, there were 40 hearths in Appleby Castle, but then only one house each with nine, eight, and six hearths, three with five, seven with four, six with three, sixteen with two and eight with one. Thirty inhabitants were exempt, many of these poorer people living in Bongate or Scattergate.

b. For Kendal the most useful account is J. F. Curwen, *Kirkbie-Kendall: fragments relating to its ancient streets and yards . . .*, 1900. Some account of life in the 'yards' appears in 'A Kendalian's Diary', a chapter in J. D. Marshall, *Old Lakeland*. A collection of newspaper articles by J. Whitwell was reprinted as *The Old Houses of Kendal* in 1866. More recently a booklet of photographs and sketches has been published by the Kendal Civic society as *A Walk Around Kendal*, 1970.

c. Carlisle was described as 'a small deserted dirty city, poorly built and poorly inhabited' in 1759 (B. C. Hutton, 'A Lakeland Journey,' *CW2*, LXI, 1961, p. 292). There had been no improvement by 1802 when Britton and Brayley found 'the dwellings of the inhabitants were mostly of wood, clay and laths exhibiting singular specimens of poverty and vitiated taste,' quoted by G. P. Jones in 'The Poverty of Cumberland and Westmorland', *CW2*, LV, 1955, p. 199. For the later transformation I am indebted to A. Harris, 'Denton Holme, Carlisle,' *CW2*, LXVII, 1967, and P. Messenger, unpublished B.Sc. thesis, University of Manchester, 1971, *Some Aspects of the Suburban Growth of Carlisle*.

7. Industrial buildings

a. Industrial development in the Lake Counties with some account of the buildings associated with the processes and houses built for industrial workers is covered in *The Industrial Archaeology of the Lake Counties*, 1970, and *The Lake District at Work*, 1971, both by J. D. Marshall and M. Davies-Shiel, in the *Lakeland Industrial Archaeology Newsletter* circulated between 1969 and 1971 by M. Davies Shiel, and in *Furness and the Industrial Revolution* by J. D. Marshall, 1958.

b. For water mills reference may also be made to J. Somervell, *Water power mills of South Westmorland*, 1930. Measured drawings of several mills by D. R. Moorhouse and in the collection of the School of Architecture of Manchester University have been very helpful.

c. G. R. Morton 'The Furnace at Duddon Bridge,' in *Journal of the Iron* and Steel Institute, June 1962, amplifies the report by T. Barlow-Massick in CW1, Vol. XIV, 1897, and has itself been amplified by Marshall and Davies-Shiel as above.

d. For textile operations, see, e.g., J. W. Kaye, 'The Millbeck Woollen Industry,' in CW2, LVII, 1958.

a. Comparative material on methods of construction, etc., may be seen in A. Clifton-Taylor, *The Pattern of English Building*, ed. of 1971, and R. W. Brunskill, *Illustrated Handbook of Vernacular Architecture*, 1970.

b. For further information on cruck construction, see F. W. B. Charles, *Medieval Cruck-Building and its Derivatives*, 1967; R. A. Cordingley, 'British historical roof types and their members,' *Transac. A.M.S.*, N.S. 9, 1961; and J. T. Smith, 'Cruck Construction: A survey of the problems,' in *Medieval Archaeology*, Vol. 8, 1964. Locally the use of cruck construction is implied in accounts of manorial customs, e.g., that of Isaac Gilpin, of mid-17C period set out in Annette Bagot, 'Mr. Gilpin and manorial customs,' *CW2*, LXII, 1962, p. 242. A collection of measured drawings of cruck-framed buildings in the region by D. R. Moorhouse is part of the drawings collection of the School of Architecture, Manchester University.

c. Further information on local techniques of clay construction appears in my article 'The Clay Houses of Cumberland' already mentioned.

d. A traveller's note on sandstone flag roof coverings and the associated roof construction appears in W. A. J. Prevost, 'A Journie to Carlyle and Penrith in 1731,' *CW2*, LXI, 1961.

8. Building construction and materials

a. For further details of doorways, etc., see M. W. Taylor, 'On Legends and inscriptions over doorways of old houses in Cumberland and Westmorland,' *CW1*, Vol. VI, 1882, and 'Some Manorial Halls in the Vale of Derwent', *CW1*, XII, 1892.

b. Reference to locks may be found in *The Lady Ann Clifford, Countess of Dorset, Pembroke and Montgomery . . .*, G. C. Williamson, 1932.

c. Many ornamental cupboards and cupboard doors, etc., are illustrated in the RCHM *Inventory* already quoted.

d. Collections of furniture, etc., are included in the National Trust properties at Hill Top, Near Sawrey (L), and Town End, Troutbeck (L) and the Lakeland Museum of Life and Industry, Abbott Hall, Kendal, all of which are open to the public.

9. Architectural detail

For accounts of the work of C. F. A. Voysey, see J. Brandon-Jones, in *Architectural Association Journal*, Vol. LXXII, May 1957; and D. Gebhard, *Introduction* to the Catalogue of the Voysey Exhibition, University of California, Santa Barbara, U.S.A., 1970.

10. Vernacular revival

The generalised distribution maps of walling and roofing materials and those illustrating the use of various plan types are based on record cards prepared for parishes or villages evenly distributed throughout the region at the rate of one to every 10 km. square on the Ordnance Survey Map and amounting in all to over 1,000 houses.

Distribution maps

Index

160